Colossians

The Treasures of Deity

Colossians

The Treasures of Deity

Dr. Bo Wagner

Word of His Mouth Publishers
Mooresboro, NC

All Scripture quotations are taken from the **King James Version** of the Bible.

ISBN: 978-1-941039-50-2
Printed in the United States of America
©2024 Dr. Bo Wagner

Word of His Mouth Publishers
Mooresboro, NC
www.wordofhismouth.com

Cover art by Chip Nuhrah

Table of Contents

Introduction

I have often observed that Colossians seems to be the wallflower of the Galatians through Colossians' Spring Formal. Galatians is where people love to go to read about the fruit of the Spirit and the prohibition against any other gospel and the law of sowing and reaping and especially the liberty that we have in Christ. Ephesians is a doctrinal gold mine, so rich in treasure that every preacher, from the youngest seminary student to the most veteran pastor, adores it. Philippians is so loaded with joy and happiness and Hallmarkesque memory verses that even the lost world often loves it without ever really even understanding it!

Colossians, though? What memory verses do you know from Colossians? If you are like most Christians, probably few or none. What messages do you hear preached from Colossians? Unless your pastor is a systematic man, probably not very many.

And yet, you simply must believe me when I tell you that Colossians is one of the richest treasure chests of the entire New Testament.

If you do not believe that by the time you are done reading this book, I will personally pray and ask the Lord to tell Paul that he needs to give you your money back for the purchase of it.

Chapter One
You Heard of Him, and We've Heard of You

Colossians 1:1 *Paul, an apostle of Jesus Christ by the will of God, and Timotheus our brother,* **2** *To the saints and faithful brethren in Christ which are at Colosse: Grace be unto you, and peace, from God our Father and the Lord Jesus Christ.* **3** *We give thanks to God and the Father of our Lord Jesus Christ, praying always for you,* **4** *Since we heard of your faith in Christ Jesus, and of the love which ye have to all the saints,* **5** *For the hope which is laid up for you in heaven, whereof ye heard before in the word of the truth of the gospel;* **6** *Which is come unto you, as it is in all the world; and bringeth forth fruit, as it doth also in you, since the day ye heard of it, and knew the grace of God in truth:* **7** *As ye also learned of Epaphras our dear fellowservant, who is for you a faithful minister of Christ;* **8** *Who also declared unto us your love in the Spirit.* **9** *For this cause we also, since the day we heard it, do not cease to pray for you, and to desire that ye might be filled with the knowledge of his will in all wisdom and spiritual understanding;*

Both in Philippians and Ephesians, we observed that Paul was in prison when he wrote them. We are going to find the same thing to be true of the book of Colossians. These three books, along with the book of Philemon, are commonly referred to as the prison epistles.

Colossians seems to have been written somewhere around AD 59-60. And it is a bit unique in that it was written to people that Paul had never met. When he wrote to the church at Philippi, he was writing to people that he had spent quality time with and was really close to. But that was not true of the church at Colosse:

Colossians 2:1 *For I would that ye knew what great conflict I have for you, and for them at Laodicea, and for as many as have not seen my face in the flesh;*

So, Paul decided to write a letter to people he had never met or spoken to. To put it mildly, that is at least a little bit unusual. But there was a reason for it, and it all centered around the deity of Christ. This short epistle will delve into that topic perhaps more fully than any other epistle.

And that is why I call this book *The Treasures of Deity.*

Breaking the ice

Colossians 1:1 *Paul, an apostle of Jesus Christ by the will of God, and Timotheus our brother,* **2** *To the saints and faithful brethren in Christ which are at Colosse: Grace be unto you, and peace, from God our Father and the Lord Jesus Christ.*

In the very first sentence of the book, Paul lets all of us know the geographical location and the people to whom this epistle was sent. This letter went to the city of Colosse, which was located between Laodicea and Heiropolis in the region of Phrygia, in Asia Minor. In our day, you would find all of that in modern-day Turkey.

The ancient city of Colosse has been extinct for nearly eighteen hundred years. You see, about a year after the writing of this epistle, not only Colosse but Laodicea and Hierapolis as well were destroyed by an earthquake. (Clarke, 510)

Laodicea was later rebuilt, and Colosse was later at least partially rebuilt but soon faded into oblivion altogether.

So, though no one knew it, Paul's letter arrived just in time. Had it been sent just a few months later, it would have arrived just in time to be lost in the wreckage of what once was Colosse, and we would not have access to this fantastic treatise on the deity of Christ.

Aren't you glad that God is never late?

Notice how Paul introduced himself to the church at Colosse:

Colossians 1:1 *Paul, an apostle of Jesus Christ by the will of God, and Timotheus our brother,*

This is not an uncommon type of greeting for Paul; it largely mirrors a great many of his epistles. He calls himself an Apostle of Jesus Christ by the will of God. The word apostle indicates one who had been sent with a message from someone else. And as we have observed from other New Testament books, an Apostle of Christ had to have seen Christ after His resurrection.

The apostle was a very special and powerful gift that Christ gave for exactly one generation at the beginning of the New Testament church. And Paul was an apostle not by his will (it was the last thing he would have ever wanted) nor by the will of others (neither those for Christ or against Christ would have wanted Paul to be an apostle) but by the will of God. Anything we do for God, even those things far less lofty than the position of an apostle, must be His will, His choice, not ours.

One last thing that Paul mentioned in verse one to the Colossians was that he was with Timothy. Timothy was well known to the early church by this point, having been taken under Paul's wing and traveling with him nearly everywhere.

And now, notice how Paul addressed the members of the church at Colosse themselves:

Colossians 1:2 *To the saints and faithful brethren in Christ which are at Colosse...*

These were not two different groups of people; they were two descriptive terms for the same group of people. They were saints, and they were faithful brethren in Christ. When we use the word saint in our day, we almost universally think of it in terms of outstanding moral behavior, so much so that it is often used derogatorily! But when it is used in the New Testament, it simply indicates those who have been saved. When God makes us a new creature in Christ at the moment of salvation, we become saints.

But that second term, faithful brethren in Christ, goes much further. It indicates those whose lives are marked by true faith and belief; it indicates actual Christians.

All Christians are saved, but not all the saved are truly Christians.

The Colossian believers were truly Christians, at least those whom Paul had in mind when he penned this epistle.

Now notice what Paul wished for them right at the outset:

Colossians 1:2b *...Grace be unto you, and peace, from God our Father and the Lord Jesus Christ.*

These words are pretty much identical to what Paul said to the church at Galatia:

Galatians 1:3 *Grace be to you and peace from God the Father, and from our Lord Jesus Christ...*

Grace is God's unmerited favor. It is God's riches at Christ's expense. It is God giving us what we do not deserve. The Greek word *xaris* that it comes from indicates that which brings delight, joy, loveliness, pleasure, sweetness, and charm.

Those are general definitions. Here are some specifics:

Grace is God the Father and God the Son looking through time before the world ever was, seeing the mess that we would make if They created us, and making us anyway. Grace is the fact that before there ever was an Eden, God had decided that there would also be a Calvary. Grace is the fact that before there ever was an accuser of the brethren, Jesus determined to be our advocate with the Father.

The second thing Paul wanted for the Colossians was peace. The world cannot seem to understand that in our lost estate, we are the enemies of God, not the children of God. Someone had to make peace, and the only one who could do it was the stronger of the two parties. The weaker party can ask for peace, but only the stronger party can make peace. And thank God He did:

Romans 5:1 *Therefore being justified by faith, we have peace with God through our Lord Jesus Christ:*

We did not even have the sense to ask for peace, but God loved us enough to offer it to us and make it possible through the blood of His own Son.

Colossians 1:3 *We give thanks to God and the Father of our Lord Jesus Christ, praying always for you,* **4** *Since we heard of your faith in Christ Jesus, and of the love which ye have to all the saints,*

Paul prayed and gave thanks for the believers in Ephesus (Ephesians 1:16), Thessalonica (1 Thessalonians 1:2), Philippi (Philippians 1:3) and now in Colosse. He was grateful for other believers! It would do us well to resurrect that spirit in our own day, a day in which believers often act like other believers are the enemy rather than the ally.

In verse four, we find the first indication that Paul did not actually know these dear people. They had heard the gospel and gotten saved under someone else's ministry. Paul had not seen their faith in Christ and love for the saints; he had heard of it, apparently from Epaphras, which is a shortened form of the name Epaphroditus. And again, what he heard was good. He heard of their faith in Christ Jesus and of the love they had for all the saints. They were that breed of radical Christian who not only had faith in Christ but also true, unfeigned love for all other believers. And Paul did not mind saying so.

Bringing the fruit

Colossians 1:5 *For the hope which is laid up for you in heaven, whereof ye heard before in the word of the truth of the gospel;* **6** *Which is come unto you, as it is in all the world; and bringeth forth fruit, as it doth also in you, since the day ye heard of it, and knew the grace of God in truth:*

The word that starts verse five, *for*, takes us back to the last phrase of verse four, that statement that they had love for all the saints. They had love for all the saints for, meaning because of, the hope that was laid up for them in heaven. This is talking about their salvation and their assurance that there really was a heaven and that they would really get to go. You see, when we use the word hope, it usually indicates a measure of uncertainty, usually a pretty large measure of uncertainty, as in, "I know that I am a three, at best, and have poor hygiene and no control over my flatulence, but I hope that ten will notice me and fall madly in love with me!"

But in Bible terms, hope meant a joyful expectation, kind of like when a wife got pregnant and then spent the next nine months joyfully anticipating holding her baby.

So the hope that was laid up for these Colossian believers in heaven affected their treatment of others here on earth. Since they were going to heaven with other believers later, they were determined to love those other believers now.

What psychopaths...

No, actually, what shining examples of what believers of all ages ought to be!

Now focus on the last phrase of verse five:

Colossians 1:5 *For the hope which is laid up for you in heaven, <u>whereof ye heard before in the word of the truth of the gospel;</u>*

The hope that the Colossians had was something they heard of before when someone brought them *the word of the truth of the gospel*. In other words, whatever preachers or soul winners came through Colosse and witnessed to these folks used heaven as part of that soul-winning pitch!

There are a few people in our day with very long, sharp noses (and tongues to match) who positively chafe at the idea of including heaven in our soul-winning methodology. And yet, it is one of the things that brought the Colossians to the saving knowledge of Christ. Heaven is real, hell is equally real, and both are perfectly acceptable to speak of when trying to win a sinner to Christ.

Paul just finished writing about the gospel in verse five, and now he will elaborate on it much more fully in verse six:

Colossians 1:6 *Which is come unto you, as it is in all the world; and bringeth forth fruit, as it doth also in you, since the day ye heard of it, and knew the grace of God in truth:*

This verse begins with a truly jaw-dropping phrase. By the time of the writing of this epistle, the gospel had been preached in all the world! It had not gone to everyone, but it had gone everywhere. And this was in just three decades' time! The early church in general, and Paul in particular, were possessed with getting access to the gospel to everyone; nothing less would do.

Our last several generations have fallen far behind in doing the same.

Why should the gospel be gotten everywhere? Because, as verse six says, it brings forth fruit. People get saved, and lives get changed. If we had two buttons, one of which would guarantee that all of the "right people" would immediately be elected to office around the world, and the other of which would guarantee that everyone in the entire world would hear the gospel, we would be far better served pushing the latter button rather than the former.

"Good politicians" do not always bring forth fruit, and when they do, a lot of that fruit turns out to be foul, fake, or fleeting. But the gospel always brings forth fruit, and the fruit that it brings forth is always good.

Notice how quickly it brought forth fruit in Colosse:

Colossians 1:6 *Which is come unto you, as it is in all the world; and bringeth forth fruit, as it doth also in you, <u>since the day ye heard of it, and knew the grace of God in truth:</u>*

Apparently, many of them got saved the very first time they ever heard the gospel and had someone explain the grace of God to them. *Do* people always get saved that quickly? No. *Can* they always get saved that quickly? Yes. God made it simple enough for that very thing to happen because some people do not have a long time; some people, in fact, are on their last few earthly breaths, and God wants to save them, too.

Building the bridge

Colossians 1:7 *As ye also learned of Epaphras our dear fellowservant, who is for you a faithful minister of Christ; 8 Who also declared unto us your love in the Spirit. 9 For this cause we also, since the day we heard it, do not cease to pray for you, and to desire that ye might be filled with the knowledge of his will in all wisdom and spiritual understanding;*

Verse seven is a strong indicator that Epaphras was the one who first preached the gospel to the Colossians and saw many of them saved and a church started. So Epaphras later became the tie-in between Paul and the Colossians. Epaphras became a fellow servant with Paul in the ministry. But for the Colossians, he was a *faithful minister of Christ*. And the word used here for minister is from the same word that we get the word deacon from and indicates one who is a servant.

15

So Epaphras did not just preach the gospel to them, he ministered to them, and he built a deep rapport with them through that. In that, he sets an excellent example for preachers everywhere. Scripture knows nothing of ministerial divas; it only knows of men with servants' hearts.

In verse eight, we learn that it was Epaphras who *declared unto us* [Paul and those who were with him in Rome] *your love in the Spirit.* This is the second time in just the first eight verses that Paul mentions the love the Colossians had for others, love that was produced by the Holy Spirit Himself. As we will see in the remainder of the epistle, there were some things they were really struggling with, but this one they had down pat!

The *for this cause* that begins verse nine goes all the way back to the foundational phrase in verse four, *your faith in Christ Jesus.* Since the day Paul heard of that and of the love it was producing in them, he and those with him did not cease to pray for them and to desire [meaning to beg and to crave] that they be *filled with the knowledge of his will in all wisdom and spiritual understanding.*

I love the way Qurollo describes this:

"Paul did not want these believers to be enthusiastically ignorant. He wanted them to be thoroughly acquainted with God's will and to have full knowledge in all wisdom and understanding or perception." (Qurollo, 24)

These people were saved, of that, there was no doubt. They also loved other believers, which put them way ahead of others to whom Paul had to write, who were always fighting like cats and dogs. Neither their salvation nor their love was in question. The only thing that was in question was their knowledge, wisdom, and spiritual understanding.

This tells us that while getting saved is enough to get us to heaven and loving others is enough to impress God and man, we still cannot afford to neglect thorough study and application of Biblical doctrine.

If we have the first two but not the third, we will end up on our way to heaven, loving others on the way there, but doing all kinds of damage along the way, robbing future generations of a solid foundation to stand on and losing incalculable rewards at the Judgment Seat of Christ.

Let me put it this way. We need to be saved, we need to be sweet, but we also need to be *sound*.

Chapter Two
A Deeper Look at Jesus

Colossians 1:10 *That ye might walk worthy of the Lord unto all pleasing, being fruitful in every good work, and increasing in the knowledge of God; 11 Strengthened with all might, according to his glorious power, unto all patience and longsuffering with joyfulness; 12 Giving thanks unto the Father, which hath made us meet to be partakers of the inheritance of the saints in light: 13 Who hath delivered us from the power of darkness, and hath translated us into the kingdom of his dear Son: 14 In whom we have redemption through his blood, even the forgiveness of sins: 15 Who is the image of the invisible God, the firstborn of every creature: 16 For by him were all things created, that are in heaven, and that are in earth, visible and invisible, whether they be thrones, or dominions, or principalities, or powers: all things were created by him, and for him: 17 And he is before all things, and by him all things consist. 18 And he is the head of the body, the church: who is the beginning, the firstborn from the dead; that in all things he might have the preeminence. 19 For it pleased the Father that in him should all fulness dwell;*

In the first section of verses that we covered in the book of Colossians, we saw Paul writing to people whom he had never met face-to-face. And I told you then that there was a vital doctrinal reason that he did so.

We will begin to find that reason in this section of verses.

Room for improvement

Colossians 1:10 *That ye might walk worthy of the Lord unto all pleasing, being fruitful in every good work, and increasing in the knowledge of God;* **11** *Strengthened with all might, according to his glorious power, unto all patience and longsuffering with joyfulness;*

When verse ten starts with the word *That,* you automatically know that it is pointing backward to something. In our vernacular, we would say something like "in order that." This word points back to what Paul desired for them in the last section of verse nine, the thing that he was even praying for for them. And that prayer, that desire, was that they be *filled with the knowledge of his will in all wisdom and spiritual understanding.* As I pointed out, it means that he wanted them to be not just saved and not just sweet but also sound in the faith. He wanted their brains to be right on all things doctrinal.

And now we find that the reason he wanted this was so that they *might walk worthy of the Lord unto all pleasing, being fruitful in every good work, and increasing in the knowledge of God; Strengthened with all might, according to his glorious power, unto all patience and longsuffering with joyfulness.*

Paul knew that what people think is generally the guiding force behind what they do. Get people believing right, and they will likely behave right. And that truth is reflected in these words. Believers are to walk worthy of the Lord. We have been taken from the pits of darkness and despair and brought into His family by the unfathomable sacrifice of Himself on Calvary! We are to walk worthy of all of that, worthy of the One who did it all for us as an act of grace alone.

And we are to do so *unto all pleasing,* which means that we are to only do those things that please Him, and we are to do everything we do in ways that please Him. He is to have our absolute best in everything.

The next phrase gives us an example of what pleases Him, the worthy walk of *being fruitful in every good work.* So, we are to do only good works, and we are to do all of the good works He expects of His children, and we are to do those good works in such a way that we are fruitful, productive in them. God does not expect us to simply pass the time here enjoying our trip to heaven; He expects us to serve Him well all the way there.

The next kind of worthy walk that pleases God and that He therefore expects of us is that we be *increasing in the knowledge of God.* So, not only does He expect us to serve Him well all the way to heaven, He also expects us to know Him better all the way to heaven. A day that we have not grown in our knowledge of Him is a day that should bother us on that account. And that truth is going to play prominently into Paul's main reason for writing this epistle.

The third kind of worthy walk that pleases Him is that we be *Strengthened with all might, according to his glorious power,* and the purpose for that is so that we will have *all patience and longsuffering with joyfulness.*

God did not and does not want His followers to be spiritually weak. He expects us to be strengthened with all might, according to His glorious power. In that phrase, *strengthened* and *might* both come from the same root word, *dunamis.* Paul was being intentionally repetitive; he was saying something like "being made powerful with all power." And then he added *according to his glorious power*, and that word for power is from *kratos,* meaning His, God's, force and strength and dominion.

If you are keeping score at home, Paul very clearly wanted the believers in Colosse to have superhuman spiritual strength, something that would make The Incredible Hulk wearing Iron Man's suit and carrying Thor's hammer seem like a ballerina by comparison.

Why in the world would he want them and us to be that strong? As I said, the purpose for that is so that we will have *all patience and longsuffering with joyfulness.*

Nothing takes more strength than patience and longsuffering, especially patience and longsuffering with joyfulness! When things go wrong for us, when we hurt, when we suffer, when we are done wrong, the last thing we want is to be patient and longsuffering with joy. That kind of thing does indeed take superhuman spiritual strength!

All of this tells us that the Colossians, and we as well, very much have room for improvement.

Reason for thankfulness

Colossians 1:12 *Giving thanks unto the Father, which hath made us meet to be partakers of the inheritance of the saints in light:* **13** *Who hath delivered us from the power of darkness, and hath translated us into the kingdom of his dear Son:*

Giving thanks unto the Father is another kind of worthy walk that pleases God. But Paul does not just tell them that as another list item in these verses; he also gives them reasons for that thankfulness.

It is in three related parts.

The first part is that the Father has *hath made us meet to be partakers of the inheritance of the saints in light.* That word *meet* is from the root word *hikanao,* and it means to make fit, to qualify. Let that sink in: God the Father has qualified us to be partakers of the inheritance of the saints in light. He has made us fit to be among Abraham, Joseph, Moses, David, Daniel, Jeremiah, Elijah, Elisha, John the Baptist, Peter, John the Beloved, Stephen, and more.

As to that list, there is one thing I do want to explain. You will meet some people who quibble with it, and you will even meet some who would scratch every single name off of the list from John the Baptist on back. They believe that the word saint only applies to New Testament Christians after the death, burial, and resurrection of Christ. The problem with that view is that saints is mentioned thirty-four times in the Old Testament. So, again, God the Father has made us fit to be among Abraham, Joseph, Moses, David, Daniel, Jeremiah, Elijah, Elisha, John the Baptist, Peter, John the Beloved, Stephen, and more, and that is a huge reason for us to be thankful.

The second part is that the Father has *delivered us from the power of darkness.* Before you even fully know what that means, you doubtless instinctively know that it is huge and worthy of our deepest thanks!

The word power is from *exsousia,* and it means the domain, authority, and jurisdiction. When we were lost, we were in the domain of darkness with no power to escape. Our father was the devil, our freedom was non-existent, and our future was hell. God the Father saw us in that predicament, and He delivered us from it. The text tells us that God hath, fully done deal, delivered us from that!

The third part is that God the Father has *translated us into the kingdom of his dear Son.* Translated is from the word *methistaymi*, and it means to remove from one place and to set somewhere else. So, when we got saved, God the Father said, "That's mine," then reached down into the domain of darkness, picked us up, removed us, and set us down permanently in the kingdom of His dear Son.

How could we be anything less than utterly thankful?

Recognition of Christ

Colossians 1:14 *In whom we have redemption through his blood, even the forgiveness of sins:*

From this point on, Paul is going to begin dealing with a heresy that was infecting the church at Colosse. We know it by the name Gnosticism. Let me give you a bit of a lengthy but excellent and easy-to-understand description of Gnosticism.

"Gnosticism took a number of different forms, but the various groups of Gnostics had a common belief that all matter was evil and that only that which was spirit was good. This heretical thinking came into conflict with Christianity in beliefs regarding the creation and the incarnation of the Lord Jesus Christ. It also resulted in extremes of behavior in asceticism, antinomianism, and licentiousness. John dealt with its effect on the person of Christ in his writings, and Jude dealt with its resulting licentiousness in his epistle. In addition, a Jewish element was mixed with Gnosticism in Colossians.

"How could a holy God create matter which was evil? In Gnostic thinking, He could not. Therefore, they believed that He created a being who was slightly less god than He was. This emanation or angelic being then created a second being who was slightly less god than he was. This second emanation or angelic being created a third emanation or angelic being who was slightly less god than he was, and this process continued on and on until eventually there was a being who was so far removed from God that he could create matter without contaminating God. Christ is viewed by these heretics as one of these angelic beings, somewhere in the middle between God and man. This Christ was not the Lord Jesus Christ, the second person of the Triune Godhead. He was not God but was instead a created being who had a beginning in time.

"According to the Gnostics, humanity cannot approach God directly but had to approach him through this angelic hierarchy. Likewise, God had to approach humanity by going through this angelic hierarchy. Therefore, it was necessary for mankind to worship these angelic beings in an apparent attempt to remain on good terms with them.

"Asceticism was also practiced in Colosse in that some would deny themselves any and all physical pleasures in order to make themselves holy. This is reminiscent of the modern practice of Lent, during which people afflict themselves to make themselves holy.

"Others went to the opposite extreme and threw off all restraints against sin (antinomianism), believing it to be all right to practice all kinds of sin (licentiousness) since it was only the body which was already wicked in and of itself." (Qurollo, 11-12)

That is a great description. But if you would like a simpler and easier-to-remember version of it, the Gnostics believed that anything physical and material was evil and only that which was spiritual and non-material could ever be good.

And now think of that in regard to Jesus. According to Paul and the other Christians, God had become *flesh*. To the

Gnostics, this was anathema! And yet, the truth of the incarnation of Christ is one of the foundational doctrines of the faith; without it, we cannot be saved. In verse fourteen, Paul began with the words, *In whom we have redemption through his blood.* We are saved because God became man and shed very real, very literal, very material, very physical blood on Calvary. That shed blood is what grants us redemption, the forgiveness of sins.

Colossians 1:15 *Who is the image of the invisible God, the firstborn of every creature:*

The word *image* in this verse is loaded with significance. It means *the likeness, the figure, the possessor of all of the attributes.* So in appearance and attribute, if you have seen the Son, you have seen the Father. This is exactly what Jesus Himself once said to Phillip:

John 14:9 *Jesus saith unto him, Have I been so long time with you, and yet hast thou not known me, Philip? he that hath seen me hath seen the Father; and how sayest thou then, Shew us the Father?*

Jesus did not tell Phillip that he had seen an angel or a lesser God. He told Phillip that since he had seen Him, Jesus, he had seen God the Father! This is the exact opposite of what Gnosticism taught.

But not only is Jesus *the image of the invisible God,* He is also *the firstborn of every creature.* And if we did not have the verses that follow, it would be easy to misunderstand that word and find ourselves in heresy as grievous as the Gnostics. Look quickly at the next couple of verses, then we will come back and deal with them more fully in just a bit.

Colossians 1:16 *For by him were all things created, that are in heaven, and that are in earth, visible and invisible, whether they be thrones, or dominions, or principalities, or powers: all things were created by him, and for him:* **17** *And he is before all things, and by him all things consist.*

Just from a glance at verses sixteen and seventeen, you know what verse fifteen is not saying. It is not saying that Jesus was a created being. He is, in fact, the One who created all things!

The word *firstborn* in verse fifteen is a euphemism pointing to priority and importance. In other words, He was not what the Gnostics were saying; He was not a lesser god/angelic being halfway down the line, low enough in the creation not to contaminate God by anything He did. Along with God the Father, He was and is the most prioritative and important being in the entire universe, and He is the One who created that universe for His Father!

Now let's look at verses sixteen and seventeen more closely:

Colossians 1:16 *For by him were all things created, that are in heaven, and that are in earth, visible and invisible, whether they be thrones, or dominions, or principalities, or powers: all things were created by him, and for him:* **17** *And he is before all things, and by him all things consist.*

Paul was not the only New Testament writer to broach this subject. Look how John also very eloquently put it:

John 1:1 *In the beginning was the Word, and the Word was with God, and the Word was God.* **2** *The same was in the beginning with God.* **3** *All things were made by him; and without him was not any thing made that was made.*

Everything in our entire universe, Jesus made it all, things that are in heaven and that are in earth, visible and invisible. He made our land and our seas and our mountains and our valleys, and He also made the angels and the throne of God and the street of gold and the Tree of Life. He made the stars and trees and animals that we can see and the atoms and molecules and magnetism and gravity that we cannot.

He also created thrones and dominions and principalities and powers. In this verse, these are four terms for classifications and hierarchies of angelic beings. Paul was pointing out that Jesus was not one of those; He had, in fact, created all of those. From the highest archangel that chose rightly and stayed to the lowest angel that chose wrongly and fell, Jesus created all of them and was not any of them.

Paul ends verse sixteen by saying, *all things were created by him, and for him.*

Everything that is, is because Christ made it. That includes me, and it includes you. And none of it was created as

26

a throwaway or an afterthought; He created everything and everyone for Him, for Himself.

You who are not sure you have a reason to live? God the Son made a you because He specifically wanted there to be a you. The same God that made Heaven and the angel Gabriel and the Milky Way and the rings of Saturn and Mount Everest and coffee beans also made you.

Notice again what verse seventeen says:

Colossians 1:17 *And he is before all things, and by him all things consist.*

That word before, from the little preposition *pro*, means before in relation to time since He created all things, and therefore nothing existed before Him. But it also means before in relation to priority, since He is the Creator rather than a part of the creation.

That last phrase, *and by him all things consist,* is stunning when you consider its scope. Consist is from the word *sunestaykan.* The prefix *sun* indicates togetherness, cohesion. The word in this verse means endures, maintains, holds together.

All things. All things are continuing to hold together because Jesus, the One who created all things, is holding those all things together.

Two hundred fifty thousand miles from where you sit, there is a moon orbiting above you. Ninety-three million miles from where you sit, our sun is warming and giving light to the earth. 3.3 billion miles away is Pluto, the farthest planet in our solar system. If you want to go to the nearest star outside of our solar system, that would be the Alpha Centauri star cluster. It is 4.2 light years away, and light travels at 186,000 miles per second. If you wanted to travel across our entire Milky Way Galaxy, that would take you 52,850 light years.

But our Milky Way Galaxy is only one of approximately two trillion galaxies in our universe. And in those two trillion galaxies, there are an estimated 200 billion trillion stars. Our universe is incomprehensibly huge! And, to make things even more interesting, every single thing in that universe, every plant, animal, person, moon, planet, and every one of those 200 billion trillion stars, is made up of atoms that are vibrating like crazy and desperately trying to fly apart at every single moment.

And the reason none of it falls apart, the reason every plant and animal and person and moon and planet and all 200 billion trillion stars continue to hold together is because Jesus Christ, the One who made it all, constantly holds it all together.

Paul wanted the Colossians to be overwhelmed at the greatness and magnitude of Christ. He wanted them to look at the heretical Gnostic view of Christ and scoff at it as the most ridiculous thing they had ever heard.

But sometimes, we fail to take really big concepts and boil them down for everyday usage. And Paul was not going to make that mistake, as we will see in verse eighteen.

Colossians 1:18 *And he is the head of the body, the church: who is the beginning, the firstborn from the dead; that in all things he might have the preeminence.*

Realizing that Christ is to be in priority over all of creation is one thing. Realizing that He is to be in priority over the body, the church, is quite another! The Gnostics would have none of that from the real Jesus since Jesus was flesh.

But He was not just man: He was and is the God-man. He was fully God and fully man, the Creator of the universe, and the head of the church. And any church that in practice does not have Him as the head has no right to call itself a Christian church. What His written Word says is either regarded as authoritative by a church, or it is not a Christian church.

After dealing with Christ as the head of the church, the next thing Paul said in verse eighteen was, *who is the beginning.*

That word *beginning* is a truly crucial word. It is from the word *arkay,* and it means the origin, the first cause. Albert Barnes said of this that He "commences everything that is designed to uphold the order of the universe, and to save the world." (Barnes, 250)

So, just like He was and is the origin and the cause of all of our material universe and creation, He was and is the origin and cause of all that has to do with our salvation. And it is that salvation part that is primarily in Paul's view as he gives us the next phrase in verse eighteen, describing Jesus as *the firstborn from the dead.*

Qurollo's description of this word firstborn is very accurate, "The first one raised from among the dead ones never to die again." (Qurollo, 31)

Throughout the Scripture, we actually find quite a few people raised from the dead, most notably Lazarus in John 11. But all of them eventually came to an uncomfortable, "Well, here we go again," moment as they had round two of dying. But Jesus rose from the dead, never to die again, and He did so as the firstborn, which is a nod ahead to us. Just like He rose from the dead, never to die again, every last one of us who has been born again will do the exact same.

And all of this that Paul wrote of here, Jesus being the head of the body, the church, Jesus being the beginning, the firstborn from the dead, was for a purpose in the mind of the Father. And the purpose, according to the last phrase of verse eighteen, was so that in all things He, Jesus, might have the preeminence. And this once again was a dagger to the heart of the filthy Gnostic doctrine that was infecting the church at Colosse. Jesus is not an angel or some lesser god. God the Father has ordained that Jesus have the preeminence in all things.

But you should surely know that this does more than just slap down Gnostic doctrine. In fact, it is equally or more so relevant in our lives today than it was then. Jesus is still to have the preeminence in everything. He is to have the preeminence in our schedules; He is to have the preeminence in our finances; He is to have the preeminence in our educational choices; He is to have the preeminence in the way we manage our families; He is to have the preeminence in our entertainment; He is to have the preeminence in our leisure; He is to have the preeminence in our life choices.

And yet, if there is one thing that Christ normally does not have even among those who call themselves Christians today, it is the preeminence. Are there very many Christians today who can truthfully say that Christ is more important to them than travel ball, or the wishes of family, or the big game, or a chance to go hunting or fishing, or some extra overtime at work?

Are there very many Christians today who can truthfully say that Christ is more important to them than what their children think about LGBTQ or other social issues?

Are there very many Christians today who can truthfully say that Christ is more important to them than what their peers at work think?

I fear that many who call themselves Christians do not even remotely understand just how little of a priority Christ truly has in their lives and how abhorrent that is in the sight of God.

But all of that about Christ having the preeminence was likely to cause a question in the minds of the Colossians, just as it is likely to cause a question in the minds of some today. And that question is simply "Why? Why should Christ be preeminent in all things? Why is it not enough for us to regard Him as extremely important alongside of other extremely important things?" And verse nineteen will answer that question very succinctly:

Colossians 1:19 *For it pleased the Father that in him should all fulness dwell;*

In case you do not quite know what Paul meant by these words, you will not have to look far for the answer:

Colossians 2:9 *For in him dwelleth all the fulness of the Godhead bodily.*

Was Jesus flesh and blood and bone on this earth? Absolutely. Was He therefore either not God or a lesser god? Not even close. All the while that physical blood pumped through His physical veins, all the while that oxygen filled His physical lungs, all the while that His physical feet walked on the dust of this world, one hundred percent of the fulness of the Godhead dwelt inside of Him. When we say that God walked among men, it is not hyperbole; God literally did walk among men. Jesus was fully God and fully man all at once. All people could see was what looked like a man, and yet inside of that humanity was full deity.

His human hands masked the hands that flung and measured the stars into place. His human voice overlayed the voice that caused light to come into existence simply by speaking to that non-existent light and having it nonetheless hear and obey and begin to be. God condescended to be contained in a vessel of flesh so that man could come to know Him and even more so, so that He could have a body in which to die for man.

So the question then is not whether or not He deserves some prominent position in our lives; the question is how could we ever think to give Him anything less than the absolute preeminence in our lives?

Chapter Three
Let's Get It Together

Colossians 1:20 *And, having made peace through the blood of his cross, by him to reconcile all things unto himself; by him, I say, whether they be things in earth, or things in heaven.* 21 *And you, that were sometime alienated and enemies in your mind by wicked works, yet now hath he reconciled* 22 *In the body of his flesh through death, to present you holy and unblameable and unreproveable in his sight:* 23 *If ye continue in the faith grounded and settled, and be not moved away from the hope of the gospel, which ye have heard, and which was preached to every creature which is under heaven; whereof I Paul am made a minister;* 24 *Who now rejoice in my sufferings for you, and fill up that which is behind of the afflictions of Christ in my flesh for his body's sake, which is the church:* 25 *Whereof I am made a minister, according to the dispensation of God which is given to me for you, to fulfil the word of God;* 26 *Even the mystery which hath been hid from ages and from generations, but now is made manifest to his saints:* 27 *To whom God would make known what is the riches of the glory of this mystery among the Gentiles; which is Christ in you, the hope of glory:* 28 *Whom we preach, warning every man, and teaching every man in all wisdom; that we may present every man perfect in Christ Jesus:* 29 *Whereunto I also labour, striving according to his working, which worketh in me mightily.*

In the last section of verses, particularly in verses fourteen through nineteen, Paul really began to delve into the main reason for the writing of this epistle. Through the heresy of

Gnosticism, the deity of Christ was being attacked. Christ was being pictured as some lesser emanation, some angelic type of being halfway down the line between God and man.

So Paul really bore down on the fact that in Him, Christ, dwelt all the fullness of the Godhead bodily. He was not just fully man; He was fully God at the exact same time. And Paul will now use this section of verses to deal with some of the effects of that hypostatic union, as it is called in theological terms.

The means of reconciliation

Colossians 1:20 *And, having made peace through the blood of his cross, by him to reconcile all things unto himself; by him, I say, whether they be things in earth, or things in heaven.*

In verse nineteen, Paul told us something that greatly pleased the Father. It pleased the Father that in Him, Jesus Christ, all fullness, meaning all fullness of the Godhead, should dwell. Verse twenty continues that thought of what pleased the Father. Not only did it please the Father that all the fullness should dwell in Christ, it also pleased Him that Christ made peace by the blood of His cross to reconcile all things unto Himself.

So let's examine the details of that.

In the words *having made peace through the blood of his cross,* we find an important matter of timing. The peace provided through the blood that Jesus shed on the cross came and comes before the reconciliation. God the Father made peace with fallen man through the sacrifice of His own Son. And He did this first. Fallen man did not ask for peace or reconciliation; God the Father provided that peace so that man could have the reconciliation. In simple terms, God saw people hopelessly lost and on their way to hell, people who wanted nothing to do with Him, and, in pure mercy and grace, made the most unfathomable sacrifice to make peace and provide an avenue for reconciliation.

The last half of verse twenty contains a huge promise, one that is often misunderstood and just as often explained away because of that potential misunderstanding. The words are, *by him to reconcile all things unto himself; by him, I say, whether they be things in earth, or things in heaven.*

If you were a wicked person who really enjoyed your sinful lifestyle, imagine what you could do with these words by twisting them a bit. "Jesus is going to save everyone; no matter what you or I do, absolutely no one is going to hell!" This belief, by the way, is variously called universalism or Christian universalism. There are Universalist churches, and there are churches that do not call themselves Universalist churches and yet teach Universalist doctrine.

But if that is what this verse teaches, we have a huge problem, namely the fact that a huge number of Scriptures actually say the exact opposite thing. Jesus Himself gave a horrific description of the eternal torments of hell in Luke 16:19-31, did so again in Mark 5 and Matthew 9, and in **Matthew 7:21-23** said, *Not every one that saith unto me, Lord, Lord, shall enter into the kingdom of heaven; but he that doeth the will of my Father which is in heaven. Many will say to me in that day, Lord, Lord, have we not prophesied in thy name? and in thy name have cast out devils? and in thy name done many wonderful works? And then will I profess unto them, I never knew you: depart from me, ye that work iniquity.*

So, right up front, take the idea of universalism in this verse completely off the table, because that is not what this verse teaches. But what, then, does it teach?

One of the great things about the writings of Paul is that he often repeats keywords and phrases, making it pretty easy to track his thought process. And in this passage, he does that for us yet again. Look at verses sixteen through twenty, and let's find a phrase that occurs six times in those five verses.

Colossians 1:16 *For by him were **all things** created, that are in heaven, and that are in earth, visible and invisible, whether they be thrones, or dominions, or principalities, or powers: **all things** were created by him, and for him: **17** And he is before **all things**, and by him **all things** consist. **18** And he is the head of the body, the church: who is the beginning, the firstborn from the dead; that in **all things** he might have the preeminence. **19** For it pleased the Father that in him should all fulness dwell; **20** And, having made peace through the blood of* *his cross, by him to reconcile **all things** unto himself; by him, I say, whether they be things in earth, or things in heaven.*

When you expand the scope all the way back to verse sixteen where Paul began to insert that phrase *all things,* your view very quickly expands from merely the salvation of a sinner to the restoration of the entire universe, all of heaven and earth. It is about every single thing in all of creation, not being *saved,* but being reconciled, which in this context means to be brought back into harmony. Paul will go on in later verses to focus it in on salvation, but for now, he is still dealing with Christ as deity, the Creator, and how He will once again have all of His creation perfect through what He in His flesh did on Calvary.

You see, the angels were given a perfect heaven, mankind was given a perfect universe and a perfect earth, and all of that was ruined by sin. Creation itself fell under condemnation and was marred and scarred and alienated from God. That is why Paul in **Romans 8:22** said, *For we know that the whole creation groaneth and travaileth in pain together until now.*

But all of that was reconciled by what Christ did on Calvary. The power of His blood goes deeper and farther than most people ever realize! It did not just provide the power for the salvation of a sinner but also for the restoration of the universe. Mind you, we will not see the true effects of that until the Millennial Reign of Christ and then especially the eternity that follows, but He has accomplished it, and it is coming.

So when you look at verse twenty and see the words *by him to reconcile all things unto himself; by him, I say, whether they be things in earth, or things in heaven,* just understand that Paul is presently thinking in terms of Christ as the Creator as much or more so than of Christ as the Redeemer. He is, though, about to use that thought to segue very much into a discussion of salvation.

Colossians 1:21 *And you, that were sometime alienated and enemies in your mind by wicked works, yet now hath he reconciled* **22** *In the body of his flesh through death, to present you holy and unblameable and unreproveable in his sight:*

Paul just finished writing about God's general reconciliation of all of creation. But now, he uses the words *and you* to introduce the part that matters the most to us, our reconciliation to God in salvation. The Colossians, and all of us as well, by the way, were alienated from God, enemies to God in our own minds and by our wicked works. In other words, both in our thoughts and our deeds, we were antagonistic to God, on the opposite side of the battle line from Him.

But the next phrase begins with the words *yet now*. And those words introduce both the happy result of what Christ did on Calvary and an issue of time that stands apart from what has come before it. Creation has not yet experienced the full reconciliation that will take place based on what Christ did on Calvary, but we have right now experienced the full reconciliation of salvation that takes place based on what Christ did on Calvary.

We do not have to wait until we get to heaven to be reconciled to God; we are already fully reconciled to God. And the words of verse twenty-two will once again obliterate Gnostic heresy as Paul shows how that reconciliation took place:

Colossians 1:22 *In the body of his flesh through death, to present you holy and unblameable and unreproveable in his sight:*

We have been reconciled *in the body of his flesh through death*. Look at the entire phrase altogether:

And you, that were sometime alienated and enemies in your mind by wicked works, yet now hath he reconciled in the body of his flesh through death.

This word *in* is a word of location. We were reconciled to God *in the body of his flesh*. Jesus, who became fully man while remaining fully God, physically shed His blood and died for us on Calvary, and that is the very spot, that body of Christ on the cross, where our reconciliation came to be. Jesus could have been born of a virgin and lived a sinless life and walked on water and healed the blinded eyes and raised the dead, and none of that would have helped us in the least had it stopped there. It was by the shedding of His blood and the dying of His body that our reconciliation was provided. God the Father and fallen man came together in the sacrifice that Jesus made hanging on that cross.

37

But all of this was not just to keep us out of hell. In fact, keeping us out of hell is not even the *primary* reason for what Christ did, let alone the *sole* reason. Look at the last phrase of verse twenty:

...to present you holy and unblameable and unreproveable in his sight:

Look at how Paul presented this same truth to the church at Ephesus:

Ephesians 5:27 *That he might present it to himself a glorious church, not having spot, or wrinkle, or any such thing; but that it should be holy and without blemish.*

God's primary purpose in reconciling us to Himself was not just to bring people to heaven but to make them fit for heaven. In fact, it was to make them fit for the very King of Heaven Himself. He expects, as Paul said here to the Colossians, for this reconciliation to result in us being holy and unblameable and unreprovable in God's sight.

But that begs a theological question, does it not? Is this merely positional, or is it practical as well? In other words, is this merely something on the inside that cannot be seen and is wholly dependent on Christ's righteousness being imputed to our account, or does this have any impact on how we live and in what God the Father sees in us now from day to day?

The answer is, it certainly is positional, but it does not stop there. Many believers would like for it to stop there because they are carnal and enjoy indulging their flesh, but it does not stop there.

Qurollo put it this way:

"There will undoubtedly be an official presentation of believers in heaven as holy, unblameable, and unreprovable in His sight; but the result of Christ's reconciliation is to make those whom He has reconciled holy, unblamable, and unreprovable in His sight, not only in their position in Christ but also in the way they live in the present age." (Qurollo, 35)

That truth is why the New Testament is so loaded with commands like this one:

1 Peter 1:15 *But as he which hath called you is holy, so be ye holy in all manner of conversation;* **16** *Because it is written, Be ye holy; for I am holy.*

That has nothing to do with the positional and everything to do with the practical. Its weight is not on what Christ did on Calvary; its weight is on what we do from day to day. And in light of what Paul was helping the Colossian believers to battle, this was a really crucial thing to understand, since some had taken their Gnosticism into the opposite ditch of Asceticism, the ditch of licentiousness.

The marks of reconciliation

The reconciliation that Christ provided for His created universe is unconditional and will be universal. But the reconciliation that Christ provided for fallen man comes with an if that is bigger than you may realize at first blush.

Colossians 1:23a *If ye continue in the faith grounded and settled, and be not moved away from the hope of the gospel...*

The *if* that begins this verse goes back to the last phrase of verse twenty-one, *yet now hath he reconciled.* In other words, you are reconciled **if...**

What follows is not going to be the basis for reconciliation; the basis for reconciliation was very clearly stated in verses fourteen and twenty, Christ's blood and Christ's death. What follows, then, is going to be the marks of reconciliation. In other words, if people are really saved, here is what will be true of them.

The first mark of real salvation Paul presents here is *If ye continue in the faith grounded and settled, and be not moved away from the hope of the gospel.*

If people stay in the faith and do not move away from the hope of the gospel, they are showing the marks of salvation. The gospel is the death, burial, and resurrection of Christ, which provides everything we need for salvation. The faith is the entire body of doctrine that the God who saved us has delivered to us in His Word. So if a person continues to cling to the gospel for salvation and the Word as God's authority for his life, he is demonstrating proof of salvation.

By contrast, if a person forsakes the gospel for salvation and begins to deny the Word as God's authority for his life, he is demonstrating proof that he never was saved to begin with. And this is especially relevant to our age of internet influencers who are "deconstructing their faith" and ending up as agnostics, atheists, and deniers of the authority of Scripture.

It is not that they were saved and have become lost. It is that, in spite of the millions of religious books that they sold and the millions of ungrounded followers they amassed, they were never saved for so much as a second.

The minister of reconciliation

Paul's focus is now on the gospel. And look at how he describes it, and then his ministry concerning it, as he concludes verse twenty-three.

Colossians 1:23 *...which ye have heard, and which was preached to every creature which is under heaven; whereof I Paul am made a minister;*

The Colossians got saved because they heard the gospel; they heard of the death and burial and resurrection of the Christ that the Gnostics denied was either fully God or fully man to begin with, when His death proved His full humanity and His resurrection proved His full deity.

The next thing Paul says of the gospel, though, is that it was *preached to every creature which is under heaven*. When he says this, he means the exact same thing that he said of the gospel in verse six: *Which is come unto you, as it is in all the world.* By the time of the writing of this epistle, the gospel had been preached in all the world. It was preached to every creature in general everywhere because it had been preached everywhere that all people were. And in the last half of verse twenty-three, Paul said, *whereof I Paul am made a minister.* God made Paul a minister of the gospel and entrusted him to get it to all people everywhere. And this thought is going to lead into a section of verses in which Paul begins to get very personal with the believers in Colosse.

Colossians 1:24 *Who now rejoice in my sufferings for you, and fill up that which is behind of the afflictions of Christ in my flesh for his body's sake, which is the church:*

Paul told the Colossians that he was right then rejoicing in the sufferings he was undergoing on their behalf. He had never seen them, nor had they ever seen him. And yet, all of the horrible things he was enduring were for them and for others who needed to hear the gospel.

Rejoicing in sufferings is not exactly normal, standard fare for us, now is it? And yet, if you and I suffer in the course of getting the gospel to others, we can rejoice just as Paul did. In eternity, the pain of the suffering will be gone, but the ones that we won to Christ will be right there with us forever, so we may as well start our rejoicing here and now!

The last half of verse twenty-four is really unique and truly doctrinally eye-opening:

...and fill up that which is behind of the afflictions of Christ in my flesh for his body's sake, which is the church:

Take a deep breath as you look at those words and begin to consider their meaning. Paul, in the context of physically suffering to get the gospel to the Colossians and others, said that he filled up, meaning to complete, that which is behind, that which is lacking of the afflictions of Christ.

Was Paul inferring that Christ, who had already died and risen again, was still suffering? Yes, he was. But before you accuse Paul of being a heretic, or before you accuse me of misunderstanding Paul and therefore being a heretic myself, let's take a look at the actual words of Jesus on the Damascus Road from after His resurrection.

Acts 9:4 *And he fell to the earth, and heard a voice saying unto him, Saul, Saul, **why persecutest thou me?** 5 And he said, Who art thou, Lord? And the Lord said, **I am Jesus whom thou persecutest**: it is hard for thee to kick against the pricks.*

Who exactly was Paul physically persecuting? He was persecuting believers, human beings, the church. He was causing men women and children to suffer so badly that they blasphemed, Acts 26:11. And yet, when Christ spoke to him from heaven, He told Paul that it was actually Him, Christ, who was undergoing that persecution.

When Christ's people, the children of God, suffer, He suffers. And while people without children may not understand this, people with children have no problem grasping it at all.

And now, years later, the Christ who had suffered with His people as Paul persecuted them was now suffering with Paul as he was persecuted by others.

As for Paul, why exactly would he do this? The last phrase in verse twenty-four gives us that answer, *for his body's sake, which is the church.*

As you should well remember from Ephesians 5, Christ loved the church and gave Himself for it. And because Paul loved what Christ loved, he was willing to give himself for the church as well.

Colossians 1:25 *Whereof I am made a minister, according to the dispensation of God which is given to me for you, to fulfil the word of God;* **26** *Even the mystery which hath been hid from ages and from generations, but now is made manifest to his saints:*

The *Whereof* refers back to the church. God made Paul a minister to the church, according to the dispensation of God which was given to him from God for them.

Dispensation is not a mystical word, especially not in this verse. It is from the word *oikonomian,* and it indicates stewardship or management of a matter. God had committed to Paul the management of fulfilling the Word of God to and for the church. It was his task, assigned to him by God, to preach the gospel to the church and to teach them all the doctrines of the faith. Here is how he put it when speaking to the Ephesian elders:

Acts 20:27 *For I have not shunned to declare unto you all the counsel of God.*

This ministerial task that God gave Paul on behalf of the church is described this way in verse twenty-six of our text, *Even the mystery which hath been hid from ages and from generations, but now is made manifest to his saints:*

As we have seen so many times before in Scripture, the fact that God would send the gospel into all the world and bring Jews and Gentiles together in one body and make a church out of them was a mystery, an unknown thing in times past. And yet, now it was made manifest, it was openly proclaimed, to His saints. And that truth is going to be stated even more clearly in the next verse.

Colossians 1:27 *To whom God would make known what is the riches of the glory of this mystery among the Gentiles; which is Christ in you, the hope of glory:*

To whom refers back to the saints in verse twenty-six. *Would* is from the word *thelo,* and it indicates a deep desire. It was the heart's desire of God to make known the riches of glory of the gospel among the Gentiles, those despised people who had been in darkness for millennia. And this was not a popular thing among the Jews to say or write; proclaiming this truth ultimately led to Paul's death.

But it was and is true, nonetheless. The riches of the glory of this mystery is *Christ in you, the hope of glory.* And this is not just Christ in general among the Gentile people that is being spoken of. It is Christ indwelling the individual! Christ merely among the Gentiles would not provide the hope of glory; Christ was among Gentiles like Pontius Pilate and Herod, and they are in hell nonetheless. It is Christ indwelling us through His Holy Spirit that provides for us the hope, the earnest expectation of the glory to come.

Colossians 1:28 *Whom we preach, warning every man, and teaching every man in all wisdom; that we may present every man perfect in Christ Jesus:*

The *Whom* Paul and his helpers preached refers to Christ. Here is how he put that to the church at Corinth:

1 Corinthians 1:23 *But we preach Christ crucified, unto the Jews a stumblingblock, and unto the Greeks foolishness;* **24** *But unto them which are called, both Jews and Greeks, Christ the power of God, and the wisdom of God.*

To every church, Paul preached Christ. And he did so, *warning every man, and teaching every man in all wisdom; that we may present every man perfect in Christ Jesus.*

This goes right back to the truth in an earlier verse that salvation was not primarily about keeping us out of hell but of conforming us to the image of Christ here and now. The teaching and preaching of every good preacher must go far beyond merely telling people how to be saved and must invade the hidden recesses of every heart and life with warnings, opening doors that people do not want to have opened and exposing every nook and cranny to the light of the truth of God's Word.

Colossians 1:29 *Whereunto I also labour, striving according to his working, which worketh in me mightily.*

Paul did not take the job of helping the Colossians and other believers become conformed to the image of Christ through the ministry of the Word lightly. He labored at it. He strove in it according to His, God's working, which God worked in him mightily. God was feverishly working in the heart of Paul to get this done, and Paul was feverishly working through that inner power to see it get done.

If you get the sense God was not satisfied with people simply being saved and that neither God nor Paul wanted believers to be weak and fractured and incomplete and ineffective, you are correct. God wanted His children here on earth to be a proper reflection of His great glory so that others would want what they have.

And that is still what He wants for us today.

So, *Let's Get It Together.*

Chapter Four
Enticing, But Wrong

Colossians 2:1 *For I would that ye knew what great conflict I have for you, and for them at Laodicea, and for as many as have not seen my face in the flesh;* **2** *That their hearts might be comforted, being knit together in love, and unto all riches of the full assurance of understanding, to the acknowledgement of the mystery of God, and of the Father, and of Christ;* **3** *In whom are hid all the treasures of wisdom and knowledge.* **4** *And this I say, lest any man should beguile you with enticing words.* **5** *For though I be absent in the flesh, yet am I with you in the spirit, joying and beholding your order, and the stedfastness of your faith in Christ.* **6** *As ye have therefore received Christ Jesus the Lord, so walk ye in him:* **7** *Rooted and built up in him, and stablished in the faith, as ye have been taught, abounding therein with thanksgiving.* **8** *Beware lest any man spoil you through philosophy and vain deceit, after the tradition of men, after the rudiments of the world, and not after Christ.* **9** *For in him dwelleth all the fulness of the Godhead bodily.*

In the last section of verses, Paul dealt extensively with reconciliation, namely the means of reconciliation, the marks of reconciliation, and himself as a minister of reconciliation. He pointed out all that Christ went through to give us the reconciliation and how a true believer will act because of that. He then got very personal with them in his description of what he had gone through to get them the word of that reconciliation. And that is what will segue us into the next section of thought.

45

A great conflict

Colossians 2:1 *For I would that ye knew what great conflict I have for you, and for them at Laodicea, and for as many as have not seen my face in the flesh;*

One verse earlier, Paul had written of his labor and his striving in the ministry. The word *for* that begins this verse ties this thought back to that thought. Paul said that he would, *thelo,* really wanted and wished, that they knew what great conflict he had for them. And that word for conflict is from the word *agona,* from which we get our English words agony and agonize. That is actually the same root word he used for the word striving in the last verse of chapter one. So, from a prison cell, Paul was waging a war for the hearts and minds of the believers in Colosse.

But not just the believers in Colosse; he also quite specifically mentioned them at Laodicea, and others who, like the believers in Colosse and Laodicea, had never yet seen him in person.

As for why he mentioned Laodicea along with Colosse, you should know that these two cities were only about nine miles apart, with Laodicea being just a bit to the northwest of Colosse. And the two cities and the bodies of believers in them were so closely tied together that, of the seven times in the actual text of the New Testament that Laodicea is mentioned, five of them are right here in the book of Colossians.

So because they were in that same region and so closely tied together, they were being infected with the same heretics and heresy.

Colossians 2:2 *That their hearts might be comforted, being knit together in love, and unto all riches of the full assurance of understanding, to the acknowledgement of the mystery of God, and of the Father, and of Christ;*

Speaking of the Colossians and the Laodiceans and all others who had not seen his face, Paul expressed that his desire was that their hearts might be comforted, first of all by being knit together in love. Were there doctrinal issues to deal with? Unquestionably. But unified bodies of believers are much harder to sway into heresy or bad behavior when they are knit together, closely and expertly joined, in love. And this is one of the benefits of a church not just meeting for preaching and teaching, but also for fun and for fellowship. People who love each other and love coming together are not quickly splintered and sent off into error.

But the other part of the equation must be true as well. Paul wanted them to love each other, but he also wanted them absolutely doctrinally sound. And that is why in the last half of the verse, Paul expressed his desire that their hearts might be comforted *unto all riches of the full assurance of understanding, to the acknowledgement of the mystery of God, and of the Father, and of Christ.*

Clearly, those words are a mouthful and take a bit to wrap your mind around. But believe me, it is worth the effort.

When Paul references riches here, it is his way of describing the information they had been given and were now being given again, information that he was about to summarize for them in the next phrase. Some information is worth more than all of the tangible riches in all of creation, and this information qualified and qualifies as such.

The full assurance of understanding is Paul's way of saying that they could be absolutely certain in what they had been taught, and that is what he was hoping for them.

And then comes the last phrase, which is the payoff of it all, *to the acknowledgement of the mystery of God, and of the Father, and of Christ.*

This full understanding assurance that Paul wanted them to have was the acknowledgment of the mystery of God, and of the Father, and of Christ. Many times, when we read the word mystery in the New Testament, it is talking about the fact that God wanted to bring the Gentiles into the fold of salvation and that He had preplanned that before the very foundation of the world. But in this particular case, we are looking at a different mystery. This is not the mystery of the gospel, it is the mystery of God, and of the Father, and of Christ. Albert Barnes got this one right when he said:

> "The sense plainly is, that there were
> truths now made known in the gospel to
> mankind, about the mode of the Divine existence,

which had not before been disclosed; and this 'mystery' he wished them to retain, or fully acknowledge. The 'mystery,' or the hitherto unrevealed truth, related to the fact that God subsisted in more persons than one, as 'Father,' and as 'Christ.'" (Barnes, 261)

These words in this place should make perfect sense to you now that you understand the context of the book of Colossians and the heresy that Paul was combating as he wrote from his jail cell so many miles away. Paul wanted them to understand the nature of God, namely that there was God, the Godhead, but that the one and only God consisted of three personages in one entity. We call that the Trinity, God the Father, God the Son, God the Holy Spirit, three persons yet only one God. And for people who were battling the Gnostics and their claim that Jesus was some being lesser than God but greater than man, this knowledge was essential. So essential, in fact, that Paul was undergoing a great conflict battling for that truth.

A glorious treasure

Colossians 2:3 *In whom are hid all the treasures of wisdom and knowledge.*

The words *In whom* that begin this verse refer back to Christ in the previous verse. It is in Christ that all the treasures of wisdom and knowledge are hidden. And when he uses the word hidden, he is pointing back to the fact that Jesus seemed so normal and ordinary when He walked among men. Just to look at Him, no one would have ever guessed that it was in Him that one could find all the treasures of wisdom and knowledge. But it was and is true nonetheless. And that fact played into the conflict at hand.

Remember that the Gnostics were coming around peddling their "secret knowledge and deep philosophy." In simple terms, they were pretending that they knew something that everybody else did not know, especially those rube Christians that were popping up everywhere. But in just eleven words, *In whom are hid all the treasures of wisdom and knowledge,* Paul drove a dagger into the heart of that pompous putridity. If you know Christ, you do not have access to the teachings of a good man; you have access to something much more magnificent. If you know Christ, you have access to all of the treasures of wisdom and knowledge.

All. All cosmological knowledge, all biological knowledge, all mathematical knowledge, all historical knowledge, all theological knowledge, everything. There is nothing that He does not know, nor is there anything that He ever gets wrong. So when a person gets saved, they get access to a whole lot more than heaven; they get access to all of the wisdom and the knowledge they will need on the way there as well.

A glaring danger

Why would Paul bother to write and tell the Colossians that in Him, Christ, were hidden all the treasures of wisdom and knowledge? He answers that question for us in verse four.

Colossians 2:4 *And this I say, lest any man should beguile you with enticing words.*

Paul informed the Colossians that in Him, Christ, are all the treasures of wisdom and knowledge, specifically so that no one would be able to beguile them with enticing words. The word beguile is from *paralogizaytai*, and it means to reckon wrong, to miscount, to deceive, to delude. It is the idea of someone talking smoothly and sounding very plausible and drawing people into their error so subtly that they do not even realize it. And the way they do this is through *enticing words*, which is from the word *pithanologia,* and means words designed to persuade. Not words designed to arrive at the truth; words designed to get people to whatever point you want them regardless of the truth.

To Paul, this was a glaring danger, mostly because it would not appear as dangerous to the relatively new Christians in Colosse.

Please understand that this always has and always will be the devil's methodology. In the very Garden of Eden, he attacked the newer of the two children of God, Eve, and he did so by coming across as the most credible-sounding presenter of error you would ever hear.

The devil does not mass-produce "I'm a dangerous heretic" T-shirts and send his emissaries into churches wearing them while angrily shouting theological error. Instead, he habitually cloaks his heresy and blasphemy in clerical garments worn by people who hate God and despise the Bible all while supposedly preaching the Bible and loving God. He uses enticing words to beguile the hearts of the simple.

You are far more likely to be led astray by a heretic in the pulpit than a heretic in the gutter. And any time someone subtly questions whether or not Christ was who He said He was, the Son of God and God the Son and the only way of salvation and the One who expects us to repent of our sin and receive Him as Lord, that is exactly what is happening.

Colossians 2:5 *For though I be absent in the flesh, yet am I with you in the spirit, joying and beholding your order, and the stedfastness of your faith in Christ.*

Paul had given a fairly stout warning in verse four. But in verse five, he seems to breathe a bit of a sigh of relief as he stipulates to what he already knows about the believers in Colosse. Yes, he knew that the Gnostics were trying to sway them into heresy. But even though he was absent in the flesh, imprisoned in Rome, he was also with them in spirit, meaning he was completely emotionally invested in what was happening there. And what he was able to say about that was that he was *joying and beholding your order, and the stedfastness of your faith in Christ.*

These words tell us that even though the devil was pouring out his most persuasive attacks against the truth among them, they still had order and steadfastness of faith in Christ. In other words, both in belief and behavior, they were still doing it right.

Most every church is going to come to their Colossians/Gnostic moment. They are going to come to a time when they are going to have to maintain the proper biblical beliefs and behaviors that they have always held from Scripture, or go a brand-new way more in keeping with the spirit of the age. And in every case, the requirement is going to be that we continue to hold fast to what God has revealed to us in His Word, and continue to see Christ just as we have always seen Him through the lens of Scripture.

Colossians 2:6 *As ye have therefore received Christ Jesus the Lord, so walk ye in him:* **7** *Rooted and built up in him, and stablished in the faith, as ye have been taught, abounding therein with thanksgiving.*

There is a pretty significant word in verse six, the word *received*. It is from *paralabeta*, and it means to receive, to accept, and to learn. In other words, there was a Christ Jesus the Lord, He was presented to them, and they received Him and learned Him as He was presented. And the significance of this goes beyond just "they received Christ as their Savior." The significance goes all the way to the fact that neither they nor anyone else got to "make their own Jesus;" Jesus was and is who He said He was, and they had to take Him as such.

Did the Gnostics teach that Jesus was some lesser emanation? Yes, they did. But did they have a right to teach that? No more than they or anyone else would have a right to teach something about *you* that is patently untrue.

Our world right now loves doing this. I have been saying for years that our culture has produced its very own Jesus. I often call him surfer dude Jesus, a Jesus that is perfectly fine with all sin and would never do or say anything to hurt anyone's feelings and would never send anyone to hell and would like nothing more than to chill out and have a brew with you.

But that Jesus is a created Jesus, not the received Jesus. If all you have is a created Jesus, then you do not have the saving Jesus. The only saving Jesus is the One who hated sin and demanded that people repent and died for every man's sins and will one day come back to rule the world with a rod of iron.

So notice again what Paul said:

Colossians 2:6 *As ye have therefore received Christ Jesus the Lord, so walk ye in him.*

Our walk as Christians has to be rooted in the Christ that we have received. The word *as* that begins this verse basically means, "In the same way that." So, in the same way that you received Him, walk in Him. The behavior stems from the basis. If our basis is that Christ is the holy Son of God and the Lord of our lives, it will be reflected in our life of holiness and

51

submission to His will. And Paul will go on in the next verse to describe certain aspects of that.

Colossians 2:7 *Rooted and built up in him, and stablished in the faith, as ye have been taught, abounding therein with thanksgiving.*

To be rooted means to be dug in and founded on a solid foundation, unshakable and unmovable. To be built up is the growth that comes out of all of that. We are to be solid in the doctrine of Christ as we received Him and showing the growth that comes from that. And the next phrase, *stablished in the faith, as ye have been taught*, deals with the body of doctrine known as "the faith." Jude used it in that manner in Jude 1:3.

Jude 1:3 *Beloved, when I gave all diligence to write unto you of the common salvation, it was needful for me to write unto you, and exhort you that ye should earnestly contend for the faith which was once delivered unto the saints.*

Paul did not merely want Colossian believers who were saved and skipping merrily to heaven. He wanted believers who maintained the doctrine that they had been taught, and in fact, were abounding in it. He wanted people who knew the Bible and biblical doctrine so well that the devil would not even bother wasting his time with them.

But none of this was to be done with pride; all of it was to be done, as the last word of this verse says, with thanksgiving. And that only makes sense. We received Christ rather than created Christ, and we receive the faith, the body of Christian doctrine, rather than create it. We can take credit neither for Christ nor for the Scripture, and therefore, all that we are left with is simply being eternally thankful for it.

That mention of the faith, the doctrines delivered to us, seems to have sent Paul back into warrior mode once again. Notice the very next thing that he said:

Colossians 2:8 *Beware lest any man spoil you through philosophy and vain deceit, after the tradition of men, after the rudiments of the world, and not after Christ.*

These are very pointed and powerful words; Paul was not the least bit interested in subtlety or winsomeness at this point. Paul told the believers in Colosse to beware, to constantly have

52

their eyes open and be vigilant against a very present danger, the danger that anyone would spoil them.

Spoil is a very picturesque word in this verse. We generally think of the word spoil as a fruit or vegetable slowly decaying and rotting. But this particular word is very different, and harkens back to the days of piracy, a very old criminal endeavor. It is from *sulagogone,* and it means to take captive, to haul away as booty.

Get that picture in your mind. Paul was warning them against allowing anyone to come in and, in a theological sense, tie them up hand and foot, throw them over their shoulder, and carry them away as booty from their conquest in the church.

I trust you understand that the devil still very much wants to do that today and is often very successful at it. Many times, what a church will see with their eyes is people being convinced of false doctrine and then walking out the door, when what is really happening unseen is that people have been convinced of false doctrine and the devil spiritually has them bound hand and foot and is carrying them out the door.

Look at the further description Paul gives of this danger:

Colossians 2:8 *Beware lest any man spoil you through philosophy and vain deceit, after the tradition of men, after the rudiments of the world, and not after Christ.*

This particular spoiling of formerly solid believers would be done, not through temptations to dark and wicked sin, but through philosophy and vain deceit after the traditions of man and after the rudiments [the fundamental principles] of the world.

You do understand, I hope, that the devil is just as happy getting someone out of church and away from good doctrine using philosophy as he is using pornography or using debate instead of drunkenness. If he can *take* you out with adultery, he will do it. But if he can *talk* you out using philosophy and vain deceit and the traditions of men and the rudiments of the world, he will do that, too. There are a lot of people who would never give in to the temptation to lie or cheat or steal, but they will give in to the temptation to listen to someone spout heresy as long as they do so in an impressive-sounding accent.

But the last phrase of that verse, *and not after Christ,* snaps our attention back to the fact that we are supposed to know better. Christ very plainly told us who He is and what He expects of us. If we get taken in by polished-sounding heresy, it is because we have not done our due diligence to pay attention to Christ and to the plain teachings of His Word.

Colossians 2:9 *For in him dwelleth all the fulness of the Godhead bodily.*

This is now the second time in this epistle that Paul has said something like this. Here, again, was the first:

Colossians 1:19 *For it pleased the Father that in him should all fulness dwell;*

Again, was Jesus flesh and blood and bone on this earth? Absolutely. Was He, therefore, either not God or a lesser god? Not even close. All the while that physical blood pumped through His physical veins, all the while that oxygen filled His physical lungs, all the while that His physical feet walked on the dust of this world, one hundred percent of the fulness of the Godhead dwelt inside of Him. When we say that God walked among men, it is not hyperbole; God literally did walk among men. Jesus was fully God and fully man all at once. All people could see was what looked like a man, and yet inside of that humanity was full deity.

His human hands masked the hands that flung and measured the stars into place. His human voice overlayed the voice that caused light to come into existence simply by speaking to that non-existent light and having it nonetheless hear and obey and begin to be. God condescended to be contained in a vessel of flesh so that man could come to know Him and, even more so, so that He could have a body in which to die for man.

So the reason that we should never go along with *philosophy and vain deceit, after the tradition of men, after the rudiments of the world,* is because no matter how good it sounds, it pales in comparison to following the One in whom all the fullness of the Godhead dwells bodily.

What the Gnostics were peddling was so pleasing to the pride of man, so enticing. But it was also something else:

It was wrong.

Enticing will never be good enough. If you doubt that, check and see how a rat is enjoying the poison twenty-four hours later.

Chapter Five
You Are Complete

Colossians 2:10 *And ye are complete in him, which is the head of all principality and power:* **11** *In whom also ye are circumcised with the circumcision made without hands, in putting off the body of the sins of the flesh by the circumcision of Christ:* **12** *Buried with him in baptism, wherein also ye are risen with him through the faith of the operation of God, who hath raised him from the dead.* **13** *And you, being dead in your sins and the uncircumcision of your flesh, hath he quickened together with him, having forgiven you all trespasses;* **14** *Blotting out the handwriting of ordinances that was against us, which was contrary to us, and took it out of the way, nailing it to his cross;* **15** *And having spoiled principalities and powers, he made a shew of them openly, triumphing over them in it.* **16** *Let no man therefore judge you in meat, or in drink, or in respect of an holyday, or of the new moon, or of the sabbath days:* **17** *Which are a shadow of things to come; but the body is of Christ.*

In the last section of verses, Paul dealt with the danger of the eloquent-sounding Gnostic heresy that was being foisted upon the church at Colosse. It was enticing, but it was wrong! And as he pointed out in verse nine, *For in him* [Christ] *dwelleth all the fulness of the Godhead bodily.* He will now continue examining the ramifications of that truth in the verses before us.

Our completion in Christ

Colossians 2:10 *And ye are complete in him, which is the head of all principality and power:*

Remember, please, that those who were peddling Gnostic doctrine to the Colossians and the Laodiceans and others were insinuating that they had secret knowledge others did not have, without which one could not be truly complete. But as Paul pointed out in this verse, in Christ, we are complete. In fact, we are, in the vernacular of the days of our youth, "amazingly complete."

You see, the phrase *ye are complete* is from the word *peplayromanoi,* from the root word *playraoh,* and it is in the perfect tense. It means to be filled to the brim, lacking nothing. And because it is in the perfect tense, it indicates an action that was completed in the past, is fully in force in the present, and will never not be what it is now.

So in Christ, we *have had* absolutely everything we need, *have* absolutely everything we need, and *always will have* absolutely everything we need. Neither the Gnostics nor anyone else will ever have something to add that we actually need to be complete. And as Paul observed in the last half of the verse, He, Jesus, this One in whom we are complete, *is the head of all principality and power.*

I love Qurollo's explanation of this phrase:

> "Is implies a continued state of being, a timeless truth, something which is true at all times and under all circumstances. Jesus is the head of all principality and power. He has not become the head of all principality and power, He always has been and He always will be the head of all principality and power. He is not part of the angelic hierarchy between God and man. He is fully God. The head means that He is in authority over them and that He is their superior." (Qurollo, 54-55)

So, since we are complete in Him, and since He is over all of the angels and angelic hierarchy that the Gnostics were pointing to, any attempt to make our way to God through angels makes as much sense as asking a meter maid to go to bat for you when your father is the king of England.

Our circumcision in Christ

Colossians 2:11 *In whom also ye are circumcised with the circumcision made without hands, in putting off the body of the sins of the flesh by the circumcision of Christ:*

The *In whom* that begins this verse is continuing to refer back to Jesus. Not only are we complete in Christ, we are also circumcised in Christ. But this circumcision is very different and far more significant than physical circumcision.

Please remember that, like most of the churches Paul started or ministered to or wrote to, the Colossians were primarily a body of Gentile believers. And while it is pretty common for Gentiles around the world to be circumcised these days because of the clear health benefits of that practice, it was not a common practice at all among the Gentiles of Paul's day. And this provided for a constant source of antagonism between Jewish believers and Gentile believers and even between Jewish nonbelievers and Gentile believers.

It is pretty clear from this verse that not only were the Colossians being beset by Gnosticism, but also by the Judaizers, and likely even by an odd combination of the two. And for us, it is a good thing that they were because this verse that Paul wrote to combat that error provides one of the greatest treasures and assurances to believers of every age.

The first phrase, *In whom also ye are circumcised with the circumcision made without hands,* tells us that we are dealing with something truly unique when it comes to circumcision. For thousands of years, circumcisions had been performed by the hands of man; knives had been wielded, flesh had been cut, and blood had been shed. But the circumcision described here does not involve flesh or knives or blood. This is a circumcision made without hands. This is a spiritual circumcision, something that will deal with a much bigger issue than health or ritual.

Look at the entire verse again, and let's focus on the last half of it this time.

Colossians 2:11 *In whom also ye are circumcised with the circumcision made without hands, in putting off the body of the sins of the flesh by the circumcision of Christ:*

Physical circumcision removed a small part of the body. And throughout the Old Testament, God made it clear that this was a picture of having our sins cut off and put away.

But that is all that it was: a picture. For thousands of years, babies were circumcised and then grew up to become idolaters and gossips and liars and murderers and drunks and a thousand other terrible things. People had one small part of their sinful body removed, and all the rest of it stayed intact to continue to break God's laws and God's heart. Circumcision did not remove sin, at all.

But the circumcision that we receive in Christ puts off the body of the sins of the flesh. The body; all of it. Not just a small part, but the entire body.

How in the world does that work?

You were made in the image of God. And like God, you are a tripartite being. God is made up of the Father, the Son, and the Holy Ghost. You are made up of body and soul and spirit. But those three parts of you are actually in two sections: the material and the immaterial. The body is material, the soul and spirit are immaterial. Another way to think of that is the outer man and the inner man. And we actually see it distinguished that way in Scripture:

Romans 7:22 *For I delight in the law of God after the* **inward man***: 23 But I see another law in my* **members***, warring against the law of my mind, and bringing me into captivity to the law of sin which is in my members.*

Members is from *melos,* and refers to the members of the body. So there you see the distinction between the inward man and the outward man. Now let's look one more time at what Paul said in Colossians, and it will begin to make sense to you.

Colossians 2:11 *In whom also ye are circumcised with the circumcision made without hands, in putting off the body of the sins of the flesh by the circumcision of Christ:*

When a person gets saved, Christ performs the most unique of all circumcisions inside of them. He separates the outer man from the inner man, the body from the soul and spirit. Your inner man is then sealed unto the day of redemption:

Ephesians 4:30 *And grieve not the holy Spirit of God, whereby ye are sealed unto the day of redemption.*

Just like Paul lamented in Romans seven, your outer man, your flesh, will be a constant source of battle for the rest of your life. But your soul and spirit, your inner man, is one hundred percent redeemed, one hundred percent perfect, and just as righteous as Christ Himself. And this is why true salvation is an eternal, perfect, irrevocable thing.

Will the deeds of your flesh still bring chastisement? Absolutely. Are you still subject to the present-day law of sowing and reaping? Of course. But as far as salvation goes, God performs an operation of grace that forever separates our inner man from the sins of our outer man. And one day, even the outer man will be made perfect:

Romans 8:23 *And not only they, but ourselves also, which have the firstfruits of the Spirit, even we ourselves groan within ourselves, waiting for the adoption, to wit, the redemption of our body.*

What a glorious day that will be when our outer man finally matches our inner man! But in the meantime, we can rejoice in knowing that our ridiculous flesh that causes us so many daily problems can never remove us from Christ; we are complete *in* Him and have been circumcised *by* Him.

But Paul still has one more illustration to use to show how new we are in Christ. Verse eleven ended, and how glorious of an ending it was! But the sentence Paul was writing, and the thought within it, actually continues into verse twelve.

Colossians 2:12 *Buried with him in baptism, wherein also ye are risen with him through the faith of the operation of God, who hath raised him from the dead.*

In verse eleven we saw that we are circumcised by Christ, and now Paul says that we are also *Buried with him in baptism*. Circumcision was a very old practice by the time Paul put pen to parchment, but baptism was far more modern. In fact, it is not mentioned at all in the Old Testament. So Paul brought both the old and the new to bear on the subject, the subject being what happened to us in salvation. Christ circumcised us, cutting the outer man away from the inner man. Christ also gave the church the ordinance of baptism, symbolizing the fact that we have died to what we once were, been buried, and been raised a brand-new creature in Christ just as Christ Himself was raised from the dead.

If it sounds like salvation has radically and irrevocably changed us, that is because it has.

The "old us" has been both cut off and put to death, forever buried, and the brand new us is now alive forevermore.

Our cleansing in Christ

We now come to some of the most glorious and picturesque words that ever flowed from the lips of God through the pen of man. The wonder begins in verse thirteen and continues through verse fifteen.

Colossians 2:13 *And you, being dead in your sins and the uncircumcision of your flesh, hath he quickened together with him, having forgiven you all trespasses;*

Paul is still building on the foundation he laid in the previous verses. The "old us" has been both cut off, circumcised by Christ and put to death, forever baptized/buried, and the brand new us is now alive forevermore. And now we find the remarkable truth that, despite appearance, what was cut away and discarded was not truly a living thing that became a dead thing. In fact, all of us, everything from head to toe, was in a state of spiritual deadness when we were in our sins and still attached to our old flesh. The sinner is a creature that is physically alive on the outside but spiritually dead both on the inside and the outside.

But when the dead outer man is put off, circumcised, we are quickened together with Christ. To be quickened means to be made alive. The saved are not just made alive; they are made alive with Him, Christ. And this tells us that we will be alive just as long as He is alive, which just so happens to be forever! And the thing that makes all of this possible is that Christ has *forgiven you all trespasses.*

There are some important things to take note of in that phrase. First of all, *having forgiven* is from the word

62

karisamenos, and the root of that word is the same word from whence we get the word *grace*. It indicates that God has given us a precious gift we did not deserve: forgiveness. He made us utterly clean.

The second thing to note is that this is in the aorist tense, meaning that it is not something being done; it is something that has been done. It is complete, and therefore it is something we do not have to worry about.

The third thing to note is that this applies to *all trespasses*, past, present, and even future! We are so completely clean and forgiven that the omniscient God, the God who exists independently of time, has already forgiven us of all of the things that we have not yet even thought of doing because we are not in the future yet to have those thoughts or commit those deeds.

So, if you have ever worried about driving down the highway and looking up just in time to see an eighteen-wheeler about to smash you in a head-on collision, and you unintentionally blurting out some foul word and losing your salvation in the last millisecond of your life, stop worrying. You absolutely should not say that foul word, but every one of your sins, past, present, and millisecond before death, has already been forgiven.

But Paul is not done yet, and the situation is about to get even better.

Colossians 2:14 *Blotting out the handwriting of ordinances that was against us, which was contrary to us, and took it out of the way, nailing it to his cross;*

As sinners, we had a lot that was not exactly going for us. We have already delved into the fact that our sinful flesh was a problem that had to be dealt with.

But going along with that problem was a written problem. You see, this was not just a matter of us feeling bad occasionally when we get some vague sense that we maybe could have done things better. There was actually a handwriting of ordinances against us, the law written by the very finger of God. It was "in the way," meaning in the midst, utterly obstructing us. That law had never been kept perfectly in all of history. Peter put it this way:

Acts 15:10 *Now therefore why tempt ye God, to put a yoke upon the neck of the disciples, which neither our fathers nor we were able to bear?*

That law could not save; it could only point out our condemnation:

Romans 3:19 *Now we know that what things soever the law saith, it saith to them who are under the law: that every mouth may be stopped, and all the world may become guilty before God.* **20** *Therefore by the deeds of the law there shall no flesh be justified in his sight: for by the law is the knowledge of sin.*

Mind you, though, the law did fulfill a very specific purpose:

Galatians 3:24 *Wherefore the law was our schoolmaster to bring us unto Christ, that we might be justified by faith.*

The law was ultimately designed to show us our hopeless condition and to teach us how much we needed Christ to step in and save us. To recap, then, there was a handwriting of ordinances that was very much against us. God Himself wrote it, and therefore man could never remove it. It left everyone condemned; it left everyone on their way to hell.

But the very same God who wrote that law ended up doing the most amazing thing with it. He came to where we were, became what we are, and did what we could not do: He kept the law absolutely flawlessly. And that qualified Him to be the perfect sacrifice and substitute for those who could not keep the law. So He, having kept all the law, then blotted it out on our behalf. And that word blotted means much more than just to dab at; it means to completely obliterate. It is as if in His perfect keeping thereof, He removed the words from the stones themselves along with every writing of our failure to pay so they could no longer be used against us and took it out of our way, making it no longer an obstacle to us. And then He went a step further and took those blotted writings to Calvary with Him, and in allowing Himself to be nailed to the cross, nailed that blotted ordinances of writing to His cross.

We could rightly put it this way. There was a bill due that we could never pay, and it had every one of our names on it. So Christ paid it for us, blotted out every ledger line against us, and then nailed it to the cross for the entirety of the world below and heaven above to see. It became our "paid in full" marker, written in red.

But the wonder of it all is still not quite yet complete:

Colossians 2:15 *And having spoiled principalities and powers, he made a shew of them openly, triumphing over them in it.*

This is not the first time in the text that we have seen the words principalities and powers. We saw them in singular form in verse ten as we started examining this section of verses. In both cases, they come from the root words *arkay* and *exousia,* and indicate high spiritual powers, in this case demonic powers. The Gnostics had come to Colosse peddling a belief that believers need to look to angelic beings to find a pathway to God. But Christ was and is so far above all angelic powers that He took the highest of the dirtiest of them and humiliated them all on Calvary. He *spoiled them*, meaning to strip them down and disarm them.

Calvary was not a victory for Satan; it was his death knell.

Calvary was not a defeat for Jesus; it was where He crushed the devil's head.

When Jesus cried out *It is finished!* it was a cry of triumph. Paul says here that Jesus *made a shew of them* [principalities and powers] *openly, triumphing over them in it.*

When Paul says that Jesus made a show of them in what He did on Calvary, the word he uses is both powerful and enjoyable to consider. The phrase *He made a shew of them* comes from the word *deigmatidzo,* and it means to make an example of. Have you ever seen a parent scoop up a rebellious toddler who was leading the smaller toddlers astray and paddle that child so that both he and the others watching him would learn a lesson? That is a good illustration of the meaning of this word.

The King paddled the devil's posterior on a hill just outside of Jerusalem.

Our cheerfulness in Christ

The spiritual basis of proper belief now covered, Paul will now quickly move into a practical outgrowth of that proper belief.

Colossians 2:16 *Let no man therefore judge you in meat, or in drink, or in respect of an holyday, or of the new moon, or of the sabbath days:* **17** *Which are a shadow of things to come; but the body is of Christ.*

The fourth word of verse sixteen, *therefore*, takes us back to the argument Paul made over the last six verses. Because the Colossian believers were complete and circumcised and clean in Christ, they were to let no man judge them in things like meat, drink, holy days, new moons, or Sabbath days. In this, Paul was taking direct aim at the oddly combined Judaizing Gnostics who not only desired to put everyone back under the law, but even went far beyond the law in claiming that preferential prohibitions must be observed for salvation, including a very long list of things one must never eat or drink. It was asceticism, a practice still widely observed in unbiblical religions around the world.

And yet, as verse seventeen observes, even the things that were in the law, things like the Sabbath, were merely shadows, or as we would say, foreshadows of things to come.

A shadow, though, no matter what casts it, no matter how big the thing that casts it, no matter how valuable the thing that casts it, still has absolutely no substance. A shadow cannot feed or water or lift anyone. We, though, have something better than a shadow. We have the body that is of Christ. We have the reality that all of the shadows pointed to. We have the relationship that all of the types tantalized us with. We have real salvation and a real relationship with the Christ who paid for it all on Calvary. And since we have all of that, we are absolutely, forever complete and are to obey the imperative command of verse sixteen and not allow anyone to judge us in any of their preferences. We are to cheerfully live our days as utterly complete Children of God, obedient to Him and His rightly applied Word, but indifferent to the snorting rebukes of people who always seem to find rules for us that neither Scripture nor the Savior ever conceived of.

We do not need people like that or their "help."

We are complete.

Chapter Six
I Just Want to Know Why

Colossians 2:18 Let no man beguile you of your reward in a voluntary humility and worshipping of angels, intruding into those things which he hath not seen, vainly puffed up by his fleshly mind, 19 And not holding the Head, from which all the body by joints and bands having nourishment ministered, and knit together, increaseth with the increase of God. 20 Wherefore if ye be dead with Christ from the rudiments of the world, why, as though living in the world, are ye subject to ordinances, 21 (Touch not; taste not; handle not; 22 Which all are to perish with the using;) after the commandments and doctrines of men? 23 Which things have indeed a shew of wisdom in will worship, and humility, and neglecting of the body; not in any honour to the satisfying of the flesh.

Paul just finished telling the church at Colosse that they had everything they needed in Christ. In Christ, they and we are complete, circumcised, cleansed, and cheerful. There is nothing lacking of what a relationship with Christ has provided for believers! And that truth will lead him into the question of these verses.

An improper worship

Colossians 2:18 Let no man beguile you of your reward in a voluntary humility and worshipping of angels, intruding into those things which he hath not seen, vainly puffed up by his fleshly mind,

69

As Paul begins, he has the subject of reward in mind. Remember, these were born-again believers to whom he was writing. As such, they did not just have heaven to look forward to; they also had rewards at the Judgment Seat of Christ to look forward to:

1 Corinthians 3:14 *If any man's work abide which he hath built thereupon, he shall receive a reward.*

And yet, the believers in Colosse were at risk of losing the very rewards that they could gain at the Judgment Seat of Christ. And they were at risk of losing them because there were people who were trying to beguile them, as verse eighteen says. That word means "to rob of a prize."

All of this comes from the picture of the ancient games at which, when a competitor ran the race and won, they would be given an award for what they did. Paul was pointing out that, while the Colossian believers were going to heaven, they were also in the process of losing out on the rewards they should be given when they got there.

So, what was causing this? This would be a good thing to know, especially if we, as believers, do not want to lose our rewards as well.

The very next phrase, *in a voluntary humility and worshipping of angels,* gives us the answer to that question. The Gnostic heretics, by their smooth-talking lies, had convinced some of the believers there in Colosse to voluntarily lower themselves in humility before angels and worship those same angels. They had done this by claiming that Christ Himself was an angel or something akin to it, some lesser emanation than God, something halfway between God and man as far as creatures go.

So, by getting them to drop their gaze from the deity of Christ to something far down the line, they were convincing them to still worship, but to worship something and someone other than God! They were saved, yet losing rewards every time they praised an angel or prayed to an angel, since that belongs only to God. And all of this, at its core, was a matter of trespassing born out of arrogance and ignorance. Look at how the last phrase of verse eighteen puts it:

...intruding into those things which he hath not seen, vainly puffed up by his fleshly mind,

Intruding. Trespassing. Going onto ground that does not belong to you. The Gnostics had never seen the spiritual world yet were quite convinced of what was there and were dragging the Colossian believers with them as they trespassed in unseen territory that did not belong to them. Rather than operating by revelation, simply trusting what God made known to man in His Word, they were "vainly puffed up" in their fleshly minds.

They thought they knew it all.

I'm just glad no one is like that today, aren't you?

Sarcasm aside, these smooth-sounding heretics, these peddlers of putrid philosophy, were robbing the Colossian believers. They were talking them out of their treasures. But if either they or the believers in Colosse had simply followed the teaching of the next verse, none of this would have ever been an issue:

Colossians 2:19 *And not holding the Head, from which all the body by joints and bands having nourishment ministered, and knit together, increaseth with the increase of God.*

Verse eighteen was what the Gnostics and those who followed them were doing. Verse nineteen is what they were not doing.

They were not *holding the head.*

By the time Paul wrote these words to the Colossians, he had already let them know what, or rather Who, the head was, twice:

Colossians 1:18 *And he is the **head** of the body, the church: who is the beginning, the firstborn from the dead; that in all things he might have the preeminence.*

Colossians 2:10 *And ye are complete in him, which is the **head** of all principality and power:*

There was, therefore, no question whatsoever that when Paul in verse nineteen accused the Gnostics and those of following them of not holding the head, he was accusing them of not holding Christ.

Holding is from the word *kratone,* and it means to lay hold of, to grasp, to seize, to hold tightly to.

If we go to heaven, it will be because Christ holds tightly to us. If we have rewards when we get there, it will be because we held tightly to Him.

And if we do hold tightly to Him, we will never fall prey to those who portray Him as something lesser than what He truly is, the Son of God and God the Son.

But this is not just a matter of rewards. Look at how the last half of verse nineteen describes the results of Him being held as the head. It says, "*... from which all the body by joints and bands having nourishment ministered, and knit together, increaseth with the increase of God.*"

In modern terms, joints and bands are the ligaments and muscles, the things that hold the body together. Those things have nourishment ministered to them by the vascular system, which sends blood to every part of the body. It is all knit together, fastened and properly working. But all of it starts with the head, the brain, which allows it all to increase with the increase of God.

In other words, it grows properly as it should when the head runs the show.

If, by chance, you had the opportunity to vote which part of your body would be in charge of all the rest, and if by chance you chose poorly, it would be a disaster in every case.

If the mouth got to be in charge (and yes, I know that for many people it seems that it is), the body would grow to grotesque size and quickly die.

If the uvula (otherwise known as the hangy-ball thing in the back of the throat) got to be in charge, everyone would walk around all day with their mouths wide open so that it could finally be seen and admired, and we would all swallow bugs and get sore throats.

There is no sensible choice other than to let the head be in charge.

Christ is the head of all powers and principalities; He is the head of the church; there is no sensible choice other than to let Him be in charge. If we are worshipping anyone but Him, even someone as glorious as an angel, it is an absolutely improper worship because only Christ is the head.

An illogical walk

Colossians 2:20 *Wherefore if ye be dead with Christ from the rudiments of the world, why, as though living in the world, are ye subject to ordinances,* **21** *(Touch not; taste not; handle not;* **22** *Which all are to perish with the using;) after the commandments and doctrines of men?*

As you read the writings of Paul, you will repeatedly note how logical of a thinker and writer he was, and that he tended to lay the foundation for proper belief in his arguments and then draw conclusions from that foundation. He does so here once again, beginning verse twenty with the word *Wherefore*. It basically means because of all that.

So, because of all the truth just laid about Christ being the head, and even going all the way back to the truth of verse twelve which shows us as having died with Christ and been raised to new life with Him, Paul had some questions for the waffling believers in Colosse.

Before we examine the question, let's define some words.

The word *if* in verse twenty is used the same way we often use it when we mean "since." It is a simple condition assumed to be true, as when we say, "If water is wet, God is good!"

The word *rudiments*, as back in verse eight of this same chapter, means fundamental principles.

The word *ordinances* means rules and regulations, in this case rules and regulations imposed by men.

The word *world* means the system of governance and philosophy laid out by the god of this world, the devil.

With all of that understood, then, Paul's question was basically this. "Since you have died with Christ to the foundational principles of this lost world, why, as if you were still lost and living in bondage to that same lost world, are you willingly being subject to its rules and regulations?"

The next phrase is parenthetical, so let's set it aside briefly and look at the main thought without it:

Wherefore if ye be dead with Christ from the rudiments of the world, why, as though living in the world, are ye subject to ordinances, after the commandments and doctrines of men?

That last phrase clearly tells us that the rules and regulations the Colossians were being pressured to subjugate themselves to were not the "thou shalts" and "thou shalt nots" of the Master, but the "dos" and "don't you dares" of man.

And now, let's look at all of that with the parenthetical phrase included, because it will let us know what those "dos" and "don't you dares" were.

Colossians 2:20 *Wherefore if ye be dead with Christ from the rudiments of the world, why, as though living in the world, are ye subject to ordinances,* **21** *(Touch not; taste not; handle not;* **22** *Which all are to perish with the using;) after the commandments and doctrines of men?*

Touch not. Taste not. Handle not. This was asceticism. This was the very long, extra-biblical list of things that one must never touch, eat, or use, things that God, neither by command nor principle, ever even mentioned. Many took it so far as to command that only dry bread could be eaten, and only water could be drunk, and only those of their particular little group of ascetics could ever even be touched.

But you can almost hear the strain in Paul's voice as he says and writes the next words, words that should be painfully obvious and logical to everyone, *Which all are to perish with the using.*

That forbidden chicken biscuit? It perishes with the using.

Please tell me you do not need me to describe that process all the way through to the end...

That forbidden milk? It perishes with the using.

Every physical thing ultimately perishes with the using. So the Gnostics were demanding that everyone follow their very, very long list concerning things that God never said a word about and were going to be consumed in the using.

And all of this made following them a very illogical waste. The Colossian believers could have been enjoying life as they held to the Head, Christ, but instead, they were now enduring life as they held to the posteriors that were directing

74

them away from the head and making them miserable all day, every day.

An insidious waste

Colossians 2:23 *Which things have indeed a shew of wisdom in will worship, and humility, and neglecting of the body; not in any honour to the satisfying of the flesh.*

The phrase chosen here to describe what the Gnostics were peddling is a good one: a shew of wisdom. They were words that gave the appearance of wisdom, words that sounded deep and philosophical and entirely plausible.

Their doctrine, first of all, had *a shew of wisdom in will worship.* That odd-sounding phrase means "worship that comes from the will of man, arbitrary worship, worship that we have designed." Worship like that, to the lost or to the carnal, will always seem to have a show of wisdom! Some of the most eloquent-sounding men in any age will be those preaching abject heresy in a lovely accent using the most well-polished of grammatical phrasing.

Their doctrine also had a show of wisdom in humility. But not proper humility directed toward God, but improper humility directed both toward their manufactured demi-god and toward the polished heretics that were peddling him.

Their doctrine also had a show of wisdom in neglecting of the body. After all, we Christians are rightly taught that our flesh is a problem. So the ascetic doctrine that taught them to deny their flesh even of the things that their flesh legitimately needed was an easy sell. This has carried over for millennia into no less a powerful organization than the Catholic Church itself, teaching people to deprive themselves of marriage and meat and conversation and a host of other right and proper things.

Their doctrine also had a show of wisdom in avoiding *any honour to the satisfying of the flesh.* Honor is from the word *timay,* and it means to place a high value upon. Once again, this one sounds almost vaguely Scriptural. If a preacher stood before you and told you not to value your flesh, you might not even bat an eye at that proclamation because, once again, the Bible generally speaks so negatively of our flesh.

But when it does so, in no case does it tell us to damage our flesh by neglect. In fact, we are told repeatedly that our body is the temple of the Holy Ghost. So even though what the Gnostics were peddling sounded so plausible, in this case, they were still dead wrong.

In all of this, they were pushing the Colossian believers to an insidious waste. They were asking them to live miserable lives, and not just miserable lives, but shortened lives due to their neglect of the body. None of this was necessary, none of it is ever necessary, since we are complete in Christ!

───────────────

There was something Paul really wanted to know. He really wanted to know why. He wanted to know why any real believers in Christ would ever fall for this and do such damage not just to themselves but also to the cause of Christ by extension. He wanted to know why believers would ever live their lives in such a weird and hurtful and needless way that the lost world would look at us as we tell them of the gospel and say, "No thanks; hard pass."

Let's be sure we never do that.

Chapter Seven
Brace Yourselves: You Are Dead

Colossians 3:1 *If ye then be risen with Christ, seek those things which are above, where Christ sitteth on the right hand of God.* **2** *Set your affection on things above, not on things on the earth.* **3** *For ye are dead, and your life is hid with Christ in God.* **4** *When Christ, who is our life, shall appear, then shall ye also appear with him in glory.* **5** *Mortify therefore your members which are upon the earth; fornication, uncleanness, inordinate affection, evil concupiscence, and covetousness, which is idolatry:* **6** *For which things' sake the wrath of God cometh on the children of disobedience:* **7** *In the which ye also walked some time, when ye lived in them.* **8** *But now ye also put off all these; anger, wrath, malice, blasphemy, filthy communication out of your mouth.*

In the last section of verses, Paul asked the believers in Colosse why they were doing what they were doing. Why, after all they had in Christ, were they willingly being subjugated to some long list of "dos" and "don't you dares" by people who claimed deep spiritual knowledge but in reality had no idea what they were talking about?

And a lot of what he argued in those verses had to do with their death and new life in Christ.

In this section of verses, he will get even more pointed about all of that.

A higher look

Colossians 3:1 *If ye then be risen with Christ, seek those things which are above, where Christ sitteth on the right hand of God.*

Much of chapters two and three of the book of Colossians bounce back and forth between the concepts of us being both dead in Christ and risen with Christ. And as chapter three begins, the opening phrase, *If ye then be risen with Christ,* takes the readers back to a phrase in verse twelve of chapter two:

Colossians 2:12 *Buried with him in baptism, wherein also ye are risen with him through the faith of the operation of God, who hath raised him from the dead.*

So, with the understanding that the word *if* in verse one is, once again, used the way that we would use the word since, Paul's argument as he begins this chapter is that since we are presently and forever already risen with Christ, we should be seeking after those things which are above in contrast to focusing on all of the long list of "below things" that supposed spiritual giants continually try to draw our attention to. All of the list of things to never touch or taste or handle were below things, not things which are above.

The last phrase of verse one, *where Christ sitteth on the right hand of God,* can easily be mistaken for filler material if we are not careful. And that would be an enormous tragedy, because they are words that are essential to the argument.

So, what was Paul inferring by this reference to Christ sitting down?

Here is how the author of the book of Hebrews put it:

Hebrews 1:3 *Who being the brightness of his glory, and the express image of his person, and upholding all things by the word of his power, when he had by himself purged our sins, sat down on the right hand of the Majesty on high;*

Hebrews 10:12 *But this man, after he had offered one sacrifice for sins for ever, sat down on the right hand of God;*

Both of those references specified that it was not until Christ had thoroughly purged our sins that He sat down on the right hand of God. In other words, as long as there was still work to do in that arena, He was up and doing it. But once the

78

redemptive work was done, He sat down since there was nothing more to do. Placed in the context of the heresy that was plaguing the church at Colosse, Paul was pointing out that there was no need to worship angels or to deprive the flesh of good and necessary things. Christ already did all of the work necessary for our redemption, and He did it so thoroughly that He was then able to simply sit down. With that being the case, why would anyone take the lower look that focuses on angels or asceticism when he could take the higher look that focuses on the assurance of full salvation in Christ?

Colossians 3:2 *Set your affection on things above, not on things on the earth.*

Set your affection is an excellent phrase. It is from the word *phroneo,* and it means to feel, to think, to cherish the same views. In other words, the whole first phrase is saying something like, "Let your mind be in love with the things above." And it is said as an imperative command, so this is a choice of the will, not just a fleeting infatuation. We are to train our mind to love heavenly, spiritual things rather than earthly, carnal things, *things on the earth.*

Many believers are undone in their walk with Christ not by some hideous sin but by a diminishing love for the above things and a growing affection for the below things. The devil is generally more shrewd than to just throw the vilest of sins in front of a person's eyes; he instead gets them little by little to lower their gaze from the things of eternal value to the things of only temporal value and from there toward the things of no value.

You need to always have a higher look.

A heavenly life

Colossians 3:3 *For ye are dead, and your life is hid with Christ in God.*

Just as verse one harkened back to a foundational phrase that Paul laid in chapter two, verse three will do the same. In chapter two, verse twenty, Paul referenced them being dead with Christ. Here, he phrases it much more abruptly, beginning by simply saying, *For ye are dead...* In fact, in the language it came from, it is even more abrupt than the characteristically smooth English we are reading here. The sentence actually starts with the word "dead." It reads like this, "Dead you are," with a heavy emphasis on the word dead. And this is why I call this section of verses *Brace yourselves, you are dead.* Because whether in our language or in their language, this is a really shocking statement. There really is no smooth way to tell someone that they are dead.

But in this case, while it cannot be smooth, it can be helpful, mostly because of what it means and because of what comes next.

What it means is that the believer is dead to his former life. Do you remember that circumcision made without hands, the *putting off the body of the sins of the flesh by the circumcision of Christ* in chapter two, verse eleven? That is what this is talking about. That old lost you has been cut off and separated from the new redeemed you. You used to be a lost inner man riding around in a lost outer man, with the inner man and the outer man joined as one. But now you are a saved inner man riding around in a lost outer man with the two forever separated, and the old lost outer you forever dead to the new saved inner you. Your old man cannot affect your position in Christ because, as far as God is concerned, it has been killed, cut off, and buried.

As to what follows, the last half of the verse says, *and your life is hid with Christ in God.*

The day you got saved, you both died and came to life. Your outer lost man died in that it was separated from your now saved inner man. But your now saved inner man came to life and is *hid with Christ in God.* In other words, just like your old sinful man can never come back to life, your new saved inner man can now never experience death. The terminology sort of paints the picture of the most divine game of hide and seek the universe has ever known. The devil is seeking your saved soul to try and destroy it, but he could never find it in ten trillion lifetimes because it is hid with Christ in God, the one place he can never go.

And to see that picture completed in the most amazing fashion, look at the next verse:

Colossians 3:4 *When Christ, who is our life, shall appear, then shall ye also appear with him in glory.*

Are you seeing it? Verse three is the divine game of hide and seek; we are *hid* with Christ in God, and the devil cannot find us. But in verse four, when He comes again, we *appear* with Him in glory. So, the devil seeks in vain for us, but we are perfectly hid with Christ in God. Then suddenly the game is up, Christ returns, and we are there with Him grinning from ear to ear at the devil who is smacking his big evil head in frustration, saying, "Agggh! No wonder I could not find them; they were all hid in Christ!" If all of this sounds like eternal security, it is because it is.

A holy lifestyle

Everything we have studied in this section of verses so far has been about what Christ did for us at the moment of salvation. But all through Scripture, we find that the story does not end there. Our position is settled; our practice is not. And writer after writer in Scripture moves from the positional, what God has done for us, to the practice, what God expects from us. And in this case, the practice was about to deal with the other side of the coin that Paul had been teaching on.

No, they were not to be ascetics.

But they were also not to swing to the other side of the pendulum and become licentious.

Colossians 3:5 *Mortify therefore your members which are upon the earth; fornication, uncleanness, inordinate affection, evil concupiscence, and covetousness, which is idolatry:*

For seventeen verses, Paul has been dealing with matters of life and death in the spiritual realm. So now, as he begins verse five, you should not have much trouble figuring out the proper definition of the word *mortify*. When we use it in our modern vernacular, we often take it to mean some great sense of embarrassment, as in, "I was simply mortified!" But this word is from the word *nekrao*, and it means to put something to death. And this once again helps us to draw a distinction between the positional and the practical.

Positionally, your flesh, your old man, has been put to death; it has been mortified, and it can cause you no further

81

problems. But practically, it is still very much alive and unmortified and causes you immeasurable problems every single day.

God is responsible for the positional; we are responsible for the practical.

Paul told them to mortify their members, which is once again from the word *melos*. It refers to the parts of the body, the flesh. Because of this, we would naturally expect the list that follows to include things like the eyes, the ears, the hands, and the mouth. But instead, the list we are given is *fornication, uncleanness, inordinate affection, evil concupiscence, and covetousness, which is idolatry*. These are the members that we are to mortify, to put to death, and the tense tells us that we are to do it thoroughly and permanently and immediately. We are not to treat this as a long process; we are to recognize these things as the works of the flesh and put them to death and bury them immediately. Our holy position demands a holy practice.

Fornication is to be put to death and buried in our lives. Fornication is a general umbrella term that means any and all sexual sin. It includes premarital sex, adultery, all forms of homosexuality, bestiality, pornography, and a great deal more. Any sexual activity outside of the bonds of a marriage between a man and his wife is absolutely off-limits and is to be ruthlessly and forever mortified out of our lives.

Uncleanness is to be put to death and buried in our lives. This is another general umbrella term that means any impurity and immorality, but once again has mostly sexual impurity in mind. Anything that God Himself would not regard as pure and right is to be ruthlessly and forever mortified out of our lives.

Inordinate affection is to be put to death and buried in our lives. This phrase refers to passions that are dirty and unnatural, and as with the first two, has mostly sexual impurity in mind. Not all affections are good and pure and right; Romans 1:26 calls some of them *vile affections*. Any twisted or perverted form of affection, anything that goes against God's pattern of intimacy only between a man and wife, is to be ruthlessly and forever mortified out of our lives.

Evil concupiscence is to be put to death and buried in our lives. This phrase means worthless lusts and cravings. Once

82

again, this phrase refers mostly to sexual impurities. But this one goes farther than the others in that it tells us that it is not just the act that is wrong; even the cravings themselves are wrong.

There is actually a fairly large and active battle over this concept in evangelical circles these days. Some pretty popular names are saying that the desires for things like homosexuality and lesbianism and pedophilia are not wrong; it is only acting on those desires that is wrong. But this misses the point that we are fallen creatures and, as such, have fallen desires. There are a great many things we want that are actually sinful. Because of that, we do not need to just be in the habit of not acting on those desires; we need to be in the habit of letting God, through His Word and the work of the Holy Spirit in our lives, transform us to the place that even those wicked desires no longer exist and find place within us. Any desire that God does not want us to have is to be ruthlessly and forever mortified out of our lives.

Covetousness, which is idolatry, is to be put to death and buried in our lives. We generally tend to think of covetousness and idolatry as two separate sins. But Paul makes it very clear that while idolatry may not always be covetousness, covetousness is always idolatry. Covetousness is the extreme desire for that which does not and should not belong to us. Covetousness makes a god out of things that we want. Covetousness is to be ruthlessly and forever mortified out of our lives.

But having all of this mortified out of our lives is not just a matter of making God happy. It will make God happy, and we should always want to do the things that make God happy. But mortifying all of these things out of our lives is actually for our own benefit as well. Look at the next verse:

Colossians 3:6 *For which things' sake the wrath of God cometh on the children of disobedience:*

These things Paul just listed, (fornication, uncleanness, inordinate affection, evil concupiscence, and covetousness, which is idolatry,) all have a consequence attached to them. All of these things that God is displeased with bring the wrath of God on the children of disobedience.

We have seen Paul use this exact same expression before in his epistle to the Ephesians:

83

Ephesians 5:6 *Let no man deceive you with vain words: for because of these things cometh the wrath of God upon the children of disobedience.*

Both in Ephesians and Colossians, children of disobedience is a pretty interesting moniker. When someone in Scripture is described as children of something or sons of something, it means that that something is their main characteristic; it is what defines them. So again, this is not just a trip or slip; this is a lifestyle. It is an indication that when people habitually do what they do, it is because they are what they are.

And when what they are is the children of disobedience, God sends His wrath on them. That being the case, no believer should want to have anything to do with any of these acts of disobedience because they are marks of the children of disobedience, not of the children of obedience, and in one way or another, there will always be a price to pay for them.

The Colossian believers were familiar both with the sins and the consequences:

Colossians 3:7 *In the which ye also walked some time, when ye lived in them.*

That list of things to mortify (fornication, uncleanness, inordinate affection, evil concupiscence, and covetousness, which is idolatry), the Colossian believers had walked and lived in those sins before they got saved. They knew the corruption, and they knew the consequences.

But Paul was still not quite done "listing."

Colossians 3:8 *But now ye also put off all these; anger, wrath, malice, blasphemy, filthy communication out of your mouth.*

The list that Paul gave in verse five dealt largely with sins of action. This list will deal largely with sins of attitude. Matthew Henry put it this way:

> "As we are to mortify inordinate appetites, so we are to mortify inordinate passions (Col 3:8): But now you also put off all these, anger, wrath, malice; for these are contrary to the design of the gospel, as well as grosser impurities; and, though they are more spiritual

wickedness, have not less malignity in them."
(Henry, 762-763)

Before we begin to examine the list, you need to understand something about Paul's opening words in verse eight, *But now ye also put off all these.* What you need to know is that these words are not a proclamation nor a prediction; they are a prescription. They do not describe what has happened or what will happen but what should happen. This is a command for them to put off all of these, meaning they were to mortify these in their lives just as they were to mortify the things on the other list in their lives. To put off is from *apotithaymi*, and it means to take off like an old rotten garment and to get rid of.

We are to put off anger, which here means hostility. A believer in Christ ought not to be a hostile individual. We are not to be the ones that end up on road rage videos or documentaries about how someone eventually shot and buried their neighbor over a disputed property line. We are not to be the ones constantly trying to tear down others online. We are not to be the ones screaming at wives and children before we come to church and earn an Oscar for how spiritual we seem. All of that is to be put off.

We are to put off wrath, which indicates emotional outbursts of ill temper. We are to be known to be levelheaded and calm and reasonable.

We are to put off malice, which means ill will. We are not to be the ones hoping for others to fall or even helping others to fall.

We are to put off blasphemy, which means injurious speech and slander. And while that often in Scripture refers to how we speak of God, everything in this context shows that the human to human relationship is what is primarily being dealt with at this point. We are not to tear others down with our words, especially not with slanderous words.

The general rule of our social media age seems to be "make an accusation first, check for the facts later." And that is a direct violation of the command of this verse. We are not to blaspheme and slander God, but we are not to blaspheme and slander others, either.

Filthy communication coming out of our mouths needs to be put away. This means words that are dirty, filthy, obscene, and improper. None of that is ever acceptable from the lips of a child of God.

To recap, there is some good news and some bad news. The good news is, you are dead. The bad news is, you are not exactly dead. Yes, positionally, your old flesh is dead and can never bother you again. But practically, it is still very much alive and will bother you every day. And because of that, you have a responsibility to put the wicked deeds of your flesh to death.

They are not to be sent into time out.

They are not to be put within proper boundaries so that you can manage them better.

They are to be mortified.

Chapter Eight
Put Off, Put On

Colossians 3:9 *Lie not one to another, seeing that ye have put off the old man with his deeds;* **10** *And have put on the new man, which is renewed in knowledge after the image of him that created him:* **11** *Where there is neither Greek nor Jew, circumcision nor uncircumcision, Barbarian, Scythian, bond nor free: but Christ is all, and in all.* **12** *Put on therefore, as the elect of God, holy and beloved, bowels of mercies, kindness, humbleness of mind, meekness, longsuffering;* **13** *Forbearing one another, and forgiving one another, if any man have a quarrel against any: even as Christ forgave you, so also do ye.* **14** *And above all these things put on charity, which is the bond of perfectness.*

Here are the words we used to summarize the last section of verses:

The good news is, you are dead. The bad news is, you are not exactly dead. Yes, positionally, your old flesh is dead and can never bother you again. But practically, it is still very much alive and will bother you every day. And because of that, you have a responsibility to put the wicked deeds of your flesh to death.

They are not to be sent into time out.

They are not to be put within proper boundaries so that you can manage them better.

They are to be mortified.

Paul will still be thinking along those same lines in this section of verses and will also be turning to some "to-dos" to go along with the "definitely don'ts."

Put off

Colossians 3:9 *Lie not one to another, seeing that ye have put off the old man with his deeds;*

Without getting bogged down in the technicalities of the grammar, please just understand that when Paul told them not to lie to one another, they were, in fact, already lying to one another. This was not a matter of "Don't ever *start* doing this;" it was "*stop* doing this." And the reason Paul gave them to stop lying to each other was that they *have put off the old man with his deeds*. So, in addition to the lists found in verse five and verse eight, that one very big and general thing they did was also to be applied to this individual specific thing they were doing.

As to the command, *lie not one to another* does not need much commentary, I would hope. We are to be truth-tellers, not liars. When we speak, people should be able to trust what we say.

The last phrase of verse nine, though, does bear some examination. Once again, it says, *seeing that ye have put off the old man with his deeds.*

In verse eight, the phrase *put off* was from *apotithaymi*, and means to take off like an old rotten garment and to get rid of. In verse nine, *put off* is from *apekduomai*, and means to strip off and renounce.

During the Cold War, people in communist countries did everything they could to escape to freedom in the West. And one group of people that had a better chance to do so than others was Olympic athletes. During the 1956 Summer Olympics, Hungarian water polo star Ervin Zador, along with dozens of others, defected to the United States. Zador gave up fame and fortune in favor of freedom and worked for $6 an hour as a lifeguard in California. Before his death in 2012, he told Sports Illustrated, "There hasn't been a moment I have regretted it." (Parker)

People like Zador took off their home country flags and home country uniforms and totally discarded them. They were nothing but worthless rags to them when compared to freedom.

That is a very good picture of the phrase used in verse nine. If a person has truly been born again, they have stripped off and renounced the old, wicked life they used to live. They have put off the old man *with his deeds.* There is not just some mystical intangible belief; there is the tangible forsaking of the things that God regards as sinful. And I truly enjoy the fact that Paul speaks here of the old man as if he were some other person entirely; *ye have put off the old man with his deeds.* Not *your* deeds, *his* deeds. You see, that old person you were before you got saved is not you anymore at all! You are someone very new and different, and therefore, his deeds no longer even belong to you and must be discarded.

A pastor had a young couple accept Christ in his church. The wife pretty quickly came to him and said, "Pastor, we need some guidance. I can't keep working my job." As it turns out, her job was to do photo shoots of sexual activity. She was making a huge amount of money doing so but understood immediately that all of that would have to be renounced, completely put off, if she was going to follow Christ.

No one ever gets saved without some understanding of the fact that Christ will expect the old sinful life to be put off. Mind you, this will be much more of a front-and-center issue in a person who is grown up and involved in horrible wickedness than it will be in a young and tender child who has never known the great depths and depravity of sin. But for those who have, there will never be an instance where a person gets saved in their old uniform of sin, waving their old flag of sin, and continues to do so. There will be repentance, or there will not be regeneration. You will renounce your sin, or you will remain in sin.

Put on

Colossians 3:10 *And have **put on** the new man, which is renewed in knowledge after the image of him that created him:*

We now come to the other side of the coin. And in any example of true salvation, both sides will be present. Not only

89

had the Colossian believers *put off* the old man with his deeds, they had *put on* the new man.

Put on is from *endusamenoi*. And just like the *put offs* in the previous verses, it uses the picture of clothing to demonstrate the truth Paul wants to communicate. It means to clothe, to put on, to wear. You see, since the day innocence was lost in the Garden of Eden, mankind, except for the very sinful or the very ignorant, has been a clothed creature rather than a naked creature. We are going to wear something; the only question is what.

The picture here is of the fact that when we were lost, we were wearing the old man and his deeds. But when we got saved, we put that off; we disrobed out of our defilement. But we cannot exactly run around spiritually naked any more than we can run around physically naked. We will have to put on something. And it every case, for every person, there are only two potential outfits in the closet. We can either put the old man back on, something that has always been dirty and is now very ill-fitting, or we can put on the new man instead. In other words, we can take the purity Christ has placed *in* us and we can put it *on* us. We can dress ourselves practically on the outside like we are spiritually on the inside. We can wear the new uniform of holiness that God has provided for us, or we can root through the dirty clothes bin and re-dress in the stained, soiled, smelly thing that we once were.

There really is only one sensible choice. And everyone will make the right choice at the moment of salvation; they will put off the old and put on the new.

It is in the days and weeks and months to follow that there will be a struggle in this area.

This new man that we are to put on is described this way at the end of verse ten, *which is renewed in knowledge after the image of him that created him:*

This new man that we put on at salvation and are to continue to put on for the rest of our lives is *renewed in knowledge after the image of him that created him.* This means that, while the sinner has a fallen and foolish mind, a mind never truly capable of understanding spiritual truths, the believer is given a renewed mind, a mind that, as in the very beginning, is once again made in God's image.

Have you ever had the frustration of arguing with a sinner about the most obvious truths? I mean things as obvious as "that wiggling child in the womb with fingers and toes and eyes and a heartbeat is a baby," to which they say, "No, it's just a clump of cells," or "It is wicked for an adult to have sex with a child" to which they say, "Pedophilia is an orientation, you bigot!"

There is no successful arguing with people like that, because their minds are broken; they do not function right. But when a person gets saved, God puts a renewed mind in them, a mind that once again has the capacity to see things as they really are.

But the sentence is not done yet; it actually starts in verse nine and continues on into verse eleven. So let's look at the entire sentence together so we can understand the full thought of verse eleven.

Colossians 3:9 *Lie not one to another, seeing that ye have put off the old man with his deeds;* **10** *And have put on the new man, which is renewed in knowledge after the image of him that created him:* **11** *Where there is neither Greek nor Jew, circumcision nor uncircumcision, Barbarian, Scythian, bond nor free: but Christ is all, and in all.*

Here is the thought. In the new man, and therefore in the mind of the new man, a mind that now once again reflects the thoughts of our Creator, there is neither Greek nor Jew, circumcision nor uncircumcision, Barbarian, Scythian, bond nor free. Instead, Christ *is all*, meaning all that really matters, the One who supersedes all previous identifies, and *in all*, meaning in every saved person no matter what they once were. And because of that, they were not to do things like lying to each other.

There was in the ancient world, just like now, this idea that we somehow owe a bit more truth and honesty to our own than to others. Many actually viewed it as perfectly acceptable to lie to others because they were "just heathens" or "just slaves." And this view seems to have even infected the church since they were, in fact, lying to each other!

The church was made up of everyone who believed – Greeks, Jews, circumcised, uncircumcised, Barbarian, Scythian, bond and free. The Jews were those descended from Abraham. The Greeks were those from the Hellenized world, people who were Greek both by birth or just by culture. Circumcised and uncircumcised are self-explanatory. Barbarians were non-Hellenized foreigners, and people in those days viewed the word Barbarian very much like we do, as a reference to savages. Scythians referred to those North and Northeast of the Caspian sea, and basically means savages that even the Barbarians thought were savages. Bond and free meant slaves and not slaves.

So the church was made up of people that, under the lost way of doing things, would have never felt the need to treat each other right; they could have lied to each other and never even bothered their consciences. But part of putting off the old man with his deeds is recognizing that Christ both *is all* and *is in all*. He is in saved Greek just like He is in saved Jews just like He is in saved circumcised people just like He is in saved uncircumcised people just like He is in saved Barbarians just like He is in saved Scythians just like He is in saved bondmen just like He is in saved freemen. So since all of them all had all that really matters, and since the Christ that is all that really matters was equally in all of them, they all mattered exactly equally and were to treat each other as such.

The early church was a glorious mish-mash of people from everywhere who all used to have an infinite number of reasons to treat each other poorly, and now all had the one reason they needed to treat each other well.

Colossians 3:12 *Put on therefore, as the elect of God, holy and beloved, bowels of mercies, kindness, humbleness of mind, meekness, longsuffering;* **13** *Forbearing one another, and forgiving one another, if any man have a quarrel against any: even as Christ forgave you, so also do ye.*

We now come to another imperative command that we put certain things on, things that are befitting our new nature. And this put on is from the same root word as the put on in verse ten, and means *to clothe, to put on, to wear*. But before we look at the list of things we are to wear in these verses, we should take note of a very essential qualifying phrase in between the command and the list, *as the elect of God, holy and beloved.* Elect means chosen, select, the best of a kind or class. It is a very regal word! And it is an indication that no less than God Himself chose us to be His own. Yes, 1 Peter 1:2 informs us that He did so based on His foreknowledge, His knowledge ahead of time that we would respond to His universal invitation to salvation, but that does not diminish the special nature of the fact that we have been *chosen.* God did not have to choose anyone to salvation. He did not even have to make the offer. Yet He made the offer to all, saw those that would receive it, and based on that knowledge, chose us as His own, not just to be saved, but to be *holy and beloved.*

He chose us to be both pure and precious in His sight.

He chose us as believers and as a bride.

He chose us as saints and special friends.

And it is on that basis that Paul now implores believers to put on several more very important things to match the change God has wrought inside of us.

We are to put on *bowels of mercies.* This means the most tender, compassionate mercies. We are to withhold from others the judgments we could rightly level on them because Christ has withheld the judgments He could rightly level on us.

We are to put on *kindness.* This means we are to be good to people and generous to people; it means we are to be nice.

We are to put on *humbleness of mind.* We are not to make ourselves big and inaccessible to people; we are to make ourselves small and approachable, like a huge adult will sometimes get down on the floor to talk to a child.

We are to put on *meekness.* This means courtesy and consideration. The meek person is the one holding the door, letting someone else have the front of the line, and noticing others rather than being fixated on self.

We are to put on *longsuffering.* This means to have a very long fuse and a capacity for taking barbs from others without feeling the habitual need to retaliate.

We are to put on the habit of *forbearing one another.* It is another way of saying, "Put up with each other." Believers come from different places with different traits with different habits, many of which are truly irritating because they are different from *my* traits and habits. But believers are to forebear; they are to put up with each other.

We are to put on the habit of *forgiving one another*. And to that one, Paul, under the inspiration of God, added this extra bit of needed commentary: *if any man have a quarrel against any: even as Christ forgave you, so also do ye.*

If any man, any of those bond/ free/ Jew/ Greek/ Barbarian/ Scythian/ circumcised/ uncircumcised have a quarrel against any of those other bond/ free/ Jew/ Greek/ Barbarian/ Scythian/ circumcised/ uncircumcised, forgive them. And do not just forgive them; identify how thoroughly and freely Christ forgave you, and you forgive them just exactly like that.

That is a big list. And yet, Paul still was not quite done; there was one more *put on* to deal with:

Colossians 3:14 *And above all these things put on charity, which is the bond of perfectness.*

Above, even more important than that really important list, higher than bowels of mercies and kindness and humbleness of mind and meekness and longsuffering and forbearing and forgiving, above even all of that, put on charity, *agapay*, true love, which is the bond of perfectness, meaning the glue that holds all of this together as a complete entity.

If you are going to be in the same body with people radically different from you and treat them with mercies and kindness and humbleness of mind and meekness and longsuffering and forbearing and forgiving, you are going to have to love them like Christ loves them and like Christ loves you. You will never simply do this out of duty; you will have to do it out of delight.

If you can put on love for the brethren, if you can make your outer man match your inner man in loving them like Christ loves them, all of this can and will be done.

So, put off, and put on.

Chapter Nine
Guided From the Inside Out

Colossians 3:15 *And let the peace of God rule in your hearts, to the which also ye are called in one body; and be ye thankful.* **16** *Let the word of Christ dwell in you richly in all wisdom; teaching and admonishing one another in psalms and hymns and spiritual songs, singing with grace in your hearts to the Lord.* **17** *And whatsoever ye do in word or deed, do all in the name of the Lord Jesus, giving thanks to God and the Father by him.*

The last section of verses dealt with the juxtaposition between the old man and the new man and the responsibility of each believer to put off certain things while putting on certain other things. Still proceeding along those same lines, these verses will use one of the smallest of words to teach one of the largest of truths.

A singular voice

Colossians 3:15a-b *And let the peace of God rule in your hearts, to the which also ye are called in one body...*

At first blush, it may seem to be no surprising thing to find the little preposition *in* mentioned twice in these verses. But let's step back and take a larger look at all three of these verses under consideration at once:

Colossians 3:15 *And let the peace of God rule **in** your hearts, to the which also ye are called **in** one body; and be ye thankful.* **16** *Let the word of Christ dwell **in** you richly **in** all*

95

*wisdom; teaching and admonishing one another **in** psalms and hymns and spiritual songs, singing with grace **in** your hearts to the Lord. **17** And whatsoever ye do **in** word or deed, do all **in** the name of the Lord Jesus, giving thanks to God and the Father by him.*

Clearly, "in" is "in" in this passage! You see, all of the putting on that we are to do on the outside is of a spiritual nature and will only have durability if it begins from the inside, where our spiritual nature resides. So with that in mind, look again at the first part of this passage under consideration:

Colossians 3:15a-b *And let the peace of God rule in your hearts, to the which also ye are called in one body...*

The *and* that begins this verse ties all the way back to the thought that began in verse nine and continued through the end of verse fourteen, namely that we are to treat other believers properly since Christ is all and is in all. If we are indeed to treat all other believers as Christ would have them treated, then the peace of God must rule in our hearts.

This verse is often more widely applied than just the immediate context and is used to guide the decision-making of a believer. And there is no real problem with that application; the word *rule* in this verse is from *brabueto*, and means to umpire, to decide as would a judge. And all of that is infinitely applicable to all of the decisions that we as believers make every single day of our lives. God should, in fact, be the one with the right to either give us peace about something or withhold that peace and have us obey His will on the matter!

That said, though, Paul was applying this truth in a bit more of a narrow fashion, as seen from the context of this passage. Remember, he has just spent several verses imploring the believers in Colosse to get along with each other and to treat each other right. And he has specifically mentioned quarrels among them just two verses earlier in verse thirteen!

When you understand all of that, and then look at the two first phrases together, *and let the peace of God rule in your hearts, to the which also ye are called in one body*, you find that what Paul is directly imploring in these words is that rather than all of the different people from different backgrounds in a church shouting and arguing and pushing to have their way, they should all instead bow to the singular voice of God, and have the peace that He brings them about each and every situation be the umpire that settles all differences.

Be honest; that doesn't sound much like the typical church, doesn't it?

The stereotypical and often well-deserved way that the world looks at the church is as a bunch of people who fuss and fight among themselves and then split and splinter like children who angrily yank their toys up and storm away to find others to play with.

But since Christ has called us together into one body, we are not to be like that at all. Adam Clarke put it this way:

> "Ye cannot have peace with God, in yourselves, nor among each other, unless ye continue in unity; and, as one body, continue in connection and dependence on him who is your only head: to this ye are called; it is a glorious state of salvation, and ye should be for ever thankful that ye are thus privileged." (Clarke, 528-529)

"Connection and dependence on him who is your only head" is an excellent way to describe the concept of the church coming together and allowing the peace of God to rule in everyone's heart.

His is to be the singular voice that settles all of our issues.

A steadying expression

Colossians 3:15c *...and be ye thankful.*

The believers in Colosse were to be putting off and putting on certain things. In that context, they were to be treating each other right no matter where they came from or what background they were of. They were to settle all of their quarrels based solely on the peace of God ruling, being the umpire in all of their hearts. But anytime anyone must make a decision or a judgment among people, the likelihood is that someone is going to be disappointed that things did not go their way, even if God is the one who has made that decision or judgment. And that is why Paul ends verse fifteen with the steadying expression, *and be ye thankful.*

Albert Barnes said of this, "An ungrateful people is commonly a tumultuous, agitated, restless, and dissatisfied people. Nothing better tends to promote peace and order than gratitude to God for his mercies." (Barnes, 279)

That is a beautiful way to put it as far as cause and effect goes. As far as the basis of this command to be grateful, though, it is very literally everything that Paul has said up to this point about Christ having paid for their sins and made them new creatures. Simply put, whether or not we get our way in any quarrel amongst ourselves, we are still to be grateful because we are redeemed and on our way to heaven. A church full of people who are willing to be grateful for that one thing that truly matters will not likely devolve into chaos over all of the smaller things that do not.

A Scriptural anchor

Colossians 3:16a *Let the word of Christ dwell in you richly in all wisdom...*

The imperative command of verse sixteen is that we let the word of Christ dwell in us richly in all wisdom. But what exactly is meant by the word of Christ in this verse? Clearly, Christ Himself is no longer physically walking among us to speak audibly in our ears, so that is not what is meant. Qurollo has the right take on this, saying, "It has to do with the entire word of God and is a statement which is intended to mean the Scripture." (Qurollo, 80)

John Wesley held the same view, saying, "So the apostle calls the whole scripture." (Linder)

William Burkitt also believed this, saying that the word of Christ is "The title given to the holy scriptures. They are the word of Christ, because they have Christ for their author, Christ for their object, and Christ for their end." (Linder)

As to how all of this ties in with what Paul has been writing about in these verses, looking at verses fifteen and sixteen together will help to make that clear:

Colossians 3:15 *And let the peace of God rule in your hearts, to the which also ye are called in one body; and be ye thankful.* **16** *Let the word of Christ dwell in you richly in all wisdom...*

Concerning the quarrels amongst them, Paul instructed in verse fifteen that the peace of God was to rule in their hearts. Verse sixteen, then, is a bit of instruction as to how to make that possible. That peace of God in our hearts does not come just from fuzzy feelings; it comes from having the Scripture *dwelling in us*. If Scripture is merely something that we hear preached and taught on Sunday, if it is merely something that we quote snippets of without even knowing where the snippets are from or what they mean, then any peace in our heart is likely to be more the product of our emotions than the umpiring call of God. But if the word of Christ is dwelling in us richly in all wisdom, meaning abundantly in broad and full knowledge and application, then God will use that to produce the very peace that settles all of our issues.

A church where each and every member studies and absorbs all of God's written Word will have the capacity, even in the hardest and hottest of issues, to retreat to what God's Word says and have Him through that bring peace to the entire situation. But a church where this is not true due to shallow, hop-skip-and-a-jump preaching or due to lazy members who expect to be spoon-fed and who do not faithfully study God's word on their own during the week will almost inevitably become a church where there is constant fighting and bickering and turmoil.

Paul knew this; hence his command to the believers in Colosse, *Let the word of Christ dwell in you richly in all wisdom.*

A singing instruction

Colossians 3:16b *...teaching and admonishing one another in psalms and hymns and spiritual songs, singing with grace in your hearts to the Lord.*

It almost seems surprising to see Paul segue into a discussion of teaching and singing at this point. But it shouldn't be; singing is one of the most powerful things we do, and when dealing with powerful problems, we need powerful help.

All of this about singing is still given in the context of the believers' need to get along and treat each other right. Did they have quarrels? Yes. And yet, since they were all one body, redeemed from all over the place and yet filled with Christ who is all and is in all, they were not to lie to each other, and they were to treat each other as family.

The peace of God ruling in their hearts would settle their quarrels. The word of Christ dwelling in them would allow the peace of God to rule in their hearts. And now we find that even their worship would contribute to their oneness.

Paul told them that they were to be *teaching and admonishing one another in psalms and hymns and spiritual songs, singing with grace in your hearts to the Lord.*

This paints such an unusual yet beautiful picture. Where the world normally expects to find a church full of people fighting like cats and dogs, Paul has painted a scenario in which a lost person could come in the doors expecting to find all of that brouhaha and instead find people literally singing to each other and teaching and admonishing each other through those songs!

Let's define some words as we begin to dig into this portion of the text.

Teaching is from the root word *didasko*. We find this same word in the second "teaching" of the Great Commission in Matthew 28:19-20. It means to instruct, to instill doctrine. It is what happens each time a Sunday school teacher or pastor systematically teaches or preaches the books and doctrines of Scripture, and it is what is happening this very moment as I am teaching you by having written this book. But it is also something that God expects us to do through our singing! Among other things, our singing is to help instruct everyone in sound biblical doctrine.

Now, to be blunt, both modern contemporary Christian music and a lot of good old-time favorites from "The Red Back Hymnal" are, quite honestly, as accurate as a blind guy with a blunderbuss when it comes to doctrine. And that is why, whether one is singing old music or new music, that music needs to be examined to see if it is even remotely scriptural.

100

Admonishing is from the root word *noutheteo,* and it means to admonish, to warn, to exhort, to instruct. In other words, think something like this in the context of all that Paul is dealing with in this passage:

(To the tune of Old Smokey)

"Now don't smack each other, for smacking is wrong, and don't trip your brother, while walking along,

Just learn to be nice, y'all; yes learn to be kind; your fussing and fighting is stressing my mind..."

Yes, I know that is a bit silly, but I hope you get the point. Our singing is to be for admonishment of one another as well as adoration of God! Brethren We Have Met To Worship is a pretty good example of a song of admonishment.

With those two words defined, notice now the three categories of singing that Paul brings to bear on this situation, *psalms and hymns and spiritual songs.*

Psalms were something the early church was very familiar with; they brought 150 of them with them from Judaism into the church. The word means *a striking, a twanging, to strike the cords of a musical instrument.* The Psalms were set primarily to stringed instruments.

Hymns comes from a word that means *to celebrate, to praise.* We tend to think of hymns as very dignified, reserved songs, but in older times they were a bit more like songs of rejoicing.

Spiritual songs were songs that pertained to the spirit, and this comes from the word *pnuematicase,* indicating wind, breath, spirit. We get our word pneumatic from it. So these were songs about spiritual things: Amazing Grace, There is A Fountain Filled With Blood, Under His Wings.

We are to communicate with each other in psalms and hymns and spiritual songs. And here is the descriptive phrase that Paul ended this instruction with:

...singing with grace in your hearts to the Lord.

Grace in this verse indicates pleasure, delight, and sweetness. We are to be singing to the Lord with delight filling our hearts. Our singing is not to be formal and perfunctory; it is to be a corporate act of worship that affects our oneness. When people sing together as they should, the music moves them from selfish individualism to selfless unity. The individual voices get lost as high voices and low voices and strong voices and weak voices blend into a unified sound.

Think about it. When people are quarreling, they instinctively raise their voices to be heard above everyone else. But when everyone focuses their hearts on God and begins to put the soprano and alto and the bass and the tenor together into a sound worthy of the King, everything changes in how people interact with each other. As good as solos can be, a good solo will never quite do this. A showy stage performance from a trio or quartet will never quite do this. Even a good choir will never *fully* do this. But when an entire church congregation puts their differences aside and delightfully worships the Lord in singing from the heart, when all of their voices blend together for the purpose, it facilitates the oneness that is needed through the worship that is jointly given.

A source of authority

Colossians 3:17 *And whatsoever ye do in word or deed, do all in the name of the Lord Jesus, giving thanks to God and the Father by him.*

In the next section of verses, Paul will begin to deal more minutely with relationships. He will move from the issue of Jews and Greeks and Barbarians and Scythians to the issue of husbands and wives and children and servants and masters. But before he does so, he ends this section of the discussion, the Jews and Greeks and Barbarians and Scythians section, with an instruction that whatever we do and whatever we say is to be done in the name of the Lord Jesus, giving thanks to God and the Father by Him.

It is clear that this is a very general statement, and needfully so. Paul was writing an epistle, not an encyclopedia. So he gives this statement to say, in so many words, "Even if it is something that I have not specifically covered, whatever you do or say, do it in the name of the Lord Jesus." What he meant by that was that all believers are to regard Christ as the head, which he has mentioned three times by this point in the epistle, and that we are therefore to obey Him and be good representatives for Him in how we treat each other. We are to do things in His name, not ours, and therefore we are to do everything His way.

The very last phrase, *giving thanks to God and the Father by him,* means that when we do whatever it is we do in His name, we are to do so giving thanks to the Father through Christ. In the context of what Paul has been discussing, we are not to treat each other well grudgingly; we are to treat each other well gratefully.

All of this is a pretty tall order. And it can only be done if we are guided from the inside out.

Chapter Ten
Outward and Upward

Colossians 3:18 *Wives, submit yourselves unto your own husbands, as it is fit in the Lord.* **19** *Husbands, love your wives, and be not bitter against them.* **20** *Children, obey your parents in all things: for this is well pleasing unto the Lord.* **21** *Fathers, provoke not your children to anger, lest they be discouraged.* **22** *Servants, obey in all things your masters according to the flesh; not with eyeservice, as menpleasers; but in singleness of heart, fearing God:* **23** *And whatsoever ye do, do it heartily, as to the Lord, and not unto men;* **24** *Knowing that of the Lord ye shall receive the reward of the inheritance: for ye serve the Lord Christ.* **25** *But he that doeth wrong shall receive for the wrong which he hath done: and there is no respect of persons.*

Colossians 4:1 *Masters, give unto your servants that which is just and equal; knowing that ye also have a Master in heaven.*

In the last chapter, I told you that in the next section of verses, Paul would begin to deal more minutely with relationships. I told you that he would move from the issue of Jews and Greeks and Barbarians and Scythians to the issue of husbands and wives and children and servants and masters.

And that is exactly what we will see and in very specific terms. And he will do so with an eye toward teaching everyone that our outward relationships with others affects our upward relationship with God.

Words for wives

Colossians 3:18 *Wives, submit yourselves unto your own husbands, as it is fit in the Lord.*

From this verse all the way through Colossians 4:1, Paul is going to follow a particular pattern in pairs. He will deal with six groups in three pairs, and in each case, he will begin with the one under authority and then deal with the one in authority. The first pair he will deal with is wives and husbands, and he begins here with the wives. The imperative command given is found in the words, *Wives, submit yourselves unto your own husbands.* He then adds a descriptive phrase to that command, *as it is fit in the Lord.*

Any reasonably proficient student of Scripture will already know that this is not the only place in Scripture where the command is given for wives to submit to their husbands. Here are some of the more notable others:

Ephesians 5:22 *Wives, submit yourselves unto your own husbands, as unto the Lord.*

Titus 2:4 *That they may teach the young women to be sober, to love their husbands, to love their children, 5 To be discreet, chaste, keepers at home, good, obedient to their own husbands, that the word of God be not blasphemed.*

1 Peter 3:1 *Likewise, ye wives, be in subjection to your own husbands; that, if any obey not the word, they also may without the word be won by the conversation of the wives;*

These are four very clear passages in Scripture delineating the wife's responsibility to submit to her own husband. Our modern world despises that, but it is every bit as Scriptural as John 3:16. But what does this command entail?

As to the command itself, the word submit is from the word *hupotassesthe*, and it means to arrange under, to yield, to subordinate oneself. It is the command that an individual who has every bit as much worth in the sight of God as the man, nonetheless, willingly obey and follow the man.

As to the descriptive phrase, *as it is fit in the Lord*, it is not a phrase that gives a loophole, as in "submit as long as that submission is fit in the Lord," though that "loophole," improperly so called, is actually Scriptural as seen in passages such as Acts 5:29. Instead, it is a descriptive phrase indicating that a wife submitting to her husband is fitting in the Lord, meaning appropriate for one who is in the Lord, appropriate for believers.

As to the extent of that requirement, as I mentioned above, Scripture is abundantly clear that no one other than God is owed absolute, unquestioned obedience. Whenever a believer, man, woman, child, or citizen is commanded to disobey God, they are to obey God. That said, unless something reaches that drastic level, wives are indeed to submit themselves to their husbands.

But we are not quite done with this verse; there is another pretty important truth it teaches that we dare not miss:

Colossians 3:18 *Wives, submit yourselves unto **your own husbands**...*

Notice those words I highlighted: *your own husbands.* That exact phrase occurred in all of the other verses I gave you earlier as well:

Ephesians 5:22 *Wives, submit yourselves unto **your own husbands**, as unto the Lord.*

Titus 2:4 *That they may teach the young women to be sober, to love their husbands, to love their children,* **5** *To be discreet, chaste, keepers at home, good, **obedient to their own husbands**, that the word of God be not blasphemed.*

1 Peter 3:1 *Likewise, ye wives, be in subjection to **your own husbands**; that, if any obey not the word, they also may without the word be won by the conversation of the wives;*

You, dear reader, are perhaps blissfully unaware of this, but there is actually a pretty vocal segment of men and even preachers in Christianity that teach that women are to be in submission to *all men.* I am not making that up; I followed a large thread of it online very recently, and there were some pretty big names espousing that foolishness. And it is foolishness; the command is very clear that the wives are to submit to their own husbands, not to some other woman's husband, and not to some single man, and not to some boy who is certain that he is a man.

Words for husbands

Colossians 3:19 *Husbands, love your wives, and be not bitter against them.*

Just as the command for the wife to submit to her own husband is found in multiple passages, so is the case with the command that the husband love the wife. Here are a few of those other notable passages:

Ephesians 5:25 *Husbands, love your wives, even as Christ also loved the church, and gave himself for it;*

Ephesians 5:28 *So ought men to love their wives as their own bodies. He that loveth his wife loveth himself.*

Ephesians 5:33a *Nevertheless let every one of you in particular so love his wife even as himself...*

In each of these passages, the word love is from the famous word *agapay,* and indicates the deepest, most self-sacrificial love. And as we see from Ephesians 5:25, it is the form of love that Christ Himself had and has for the church. Simply put, then, the husband is to love the wife just exactly as well in every regard as Christ loves the church.

Qurollo described this exceedingly well, saying:

"The husband is required by God to love his wife with a love which gives itself one hundred percent on behalf of her without expecting anything in return. Many men may be willing to love their wives if they get something in return. The believer, however, must love his wife even if he gets nothing in return." (Qurollo, 83)

Anyone who truly grasps this verse will come to the conclusion that the husband, by far, has the weightier responsibility in the relationship, as he should.

But that responsibility is not even close to being done yet. When the wife was commanded in this text to submit to her husband, there was a descriptive phrase added. Now we will find something similar in the command for the husband to love his wife. Verse nineteen ends with the words, *"and be not bitter against them."*

William Burkitt gave a fantastic explanation of this command:

> "A particular sin, which all husbands are to avoid in their conversation with their wives, [is that of] being bitter against them: not bitter in affection towards them, that is, cold and indifferent in their love to them; not bitter in expression towards them, speaking reproachfully to them; not bitter in their actions towards them, giving them bitter blows, which is contrary to the law of God and nature.
>
> "Learn hence, That it is the will and command of God, that husbands should not behave themselves churlishly, sourly, or imperiously towards their wives; not ruling with rigour or being morose and rough, stern and severe in their carriage towards them, but to treat them with that endearing familiarity that is due to them, as part of ourselves." (Linder)

Those are two fantastic and flowing paragraphs to describe the command given to the husbands at the end of verse nineteen. But may I give you a very short, accurate, to-the-point summary of those words and of the command itself?

Husbands are commanded not to be jerks.

How often, though, does this side of the coin even come up when there is an issue between a husband and wife? Anecdotally, I can tell you from what I have heard through the years that when a wife is having to live with a horse's rear end of a husband, the only one that ever gets dealt with is her. The vast majority of the time, she will be told that even though her husband is indeed a USDA-certified horse's patooty, she is required to sweetly submit to him, but at no time is he ever called on the carpet and told that he is required to stop being a jerk.

But the command for the husband to love his wife and not be bitter against her is every bit as much in the Bible as the command for her to be submissive. And (once again anecdotally) I have rarely seen a woman who was loved that way who had any problem submitting. On a few occasions, yes, but rarely, very rarely. And it is instructive to note that there is not one single command in Scripture for the wife to submit that is not immediately rounded out with the husband's command to love her with that *agapay* love. Not one. So to separate the two and only focus on the one is biblical illiteracy and ministerial malpractice.

Words for children

Colossians 3:20 *Children, obey your parents in all things: for this is well pleasing unto the Lord.*

We now come to the second pairing that Paul will deal with, children and fathers, and he will start with the children. As with the previous two commands, this one has been seen elsewhere in Scripture. Here is one notable example:

Ephesians 6:1 *Children, obey your parents in the Lord: for this is right.*

In both of these passages, obey is from the root word *hupacouo*. It is a compound word, the first part of which, *hupo*, means under, and the second part of which, *acouo*, means to listen or to hear. We get our word acoustic from it. So the whole word means "to listen under." It paints the picture of one listening to an authority over them and obeying what they hear.

That is not exactly the standard parent/child model in our modern day, is it! But God expects it to be. Children are indeed commanded to obey their parents, and Colossians 3:20 adds the phrase *in all things*.

Once again, that brings up the question of how far this goes. Are they to obey if their parents command them to curse God? Are they to obey if they are commanded to slice the throats of their baby siblings?

Of course not. Again, Scripture explains Scripture, and Acts 5:29 applies here as well. If a case so extreme as this ever came up, if a child was commanded to blatantly disobey God, then God must be obeyed, and man must be disobeyed. The command of Colossians 3:21 gives the rule, not the exception.

But leaving those extreme, utterly rare exceptions aside, the command of God for children is that they obey their parents in all things. They may not like the parental curfew or dress standards, or being told who they may and may not hang around, or what they can and cannot listen to, but they are nonetheless required to obey. And a parent who does not demand this of their children is helping those children to disobey God. And one of the reasons this is such a tragedy is because the end of the verse says, *"for this is well pleasing unto the Lord."* Thus, a child who does not obey is missing out on the opportunity to greatly please the Lord and on the blessings that He will send on their lives because He is so pleased by what He sees.

I have three young adult children. All of them were "made to mind" as kids. We *required* it. And they did it. Sometimes they liked it, sometimes they did not like it, but they did it. And it eventually became them doing it because they internalized it, rather than it being merely an external expectation. They made the practice theirs. And all of them have been mightily, abundantly blessed by God. It is nothing unusual at all for one of them to excitedly call during the day and say, "Guess what God just did for me!"

Parents, do not rob your children of that. Them obeying you is well pleasing to the Lord.

Words for fathers

Colossians 3:21 *Fathers, provoke not your children to anger, lest they be discouraged.*

Once again, we have seen this command in Scripture before as well:

Ephesians 6:4 *And, ye fathers, provoke not your children to wrath: but bring them up in the nurture and admonition of the Lord.*

The command of Colossians 3:21 means that fathers are not to behave in a way that leaves their children frustrated, bitter, and resentful. The reason for the command is that if the fathers behave in such a way as to provoke their children to such anger, they will become discouraged. And that is from the picturesque word *athumosin,* meaning to lose heart, to be dispirited, to give up.

As with the husband's responsibility to the wife, this is a command for a father not to be an overbearing, impossible-to-please jerk. Nothing will break a child's spirit so successfully, thoroughly, and permanently as a father like that.

Let me give you part of an email I received from one of my newspaper columns.

"Dear Mr. Wagner, my daughter struggles with the thought of God the Father. Her father is not a good father figure, and I think seeing God as a Father is what she dislikes because of the shortcomings of her own father.

"Thank you for any insights you may have."

Yes, I answered. But I also grieved. Somewhere out there is a precious girl who hates the thought of God the Father because her own father has poisoned her to that truth by his own bad behavior. So let me say here what I also said when writing the commentary on Ephesians. Fathers, yes, you must uphold the Biblical standards of right and wrong in your home. But you must also be your children's biggest cheerleader and fiercest advocate and greatest comfort and most consistent teacher.

And if you are not, if you are instead an ogre to them, you might not want to come to me with complaints about your children not obeying because I promise you, I am going to hurt your feelings.

Words for servants

Colossians 3:22 *Servants, obey in all things your masters according to the flesh; not with eyeservice, as menpleasers; but in singleness of heart, fearing God:*

We now come to the third pairing that Paul will deal with, servants and masters, and he will start with the servants. As with the previous four commands, this one is seen elsewhere in Scripture. Here are some notable examples:

Ephesians 6:5 *Servants, be obedient to them that are your masters according to the flesh, with fear and trembling, in singleness of your heart, as unto Christ;*

1 Timothy 6:1 *Let as many servants as are under the yoke count their own masters worthy of all honour, that the name of God and his doctrine be not blasphemed.*

Titus 2:9 *Exhort servants to be obedient unto their own masters, and to please them well in all things; not answering again;*

1 Peter 2:18 *Servants, be subject to your masters with all fear; not only to the good and gentle, but also to the froward.*

Both slavery and servitude were common in the Roman world. Indentured servitude was especially common. When people got into debt and found themselves with no way to pay, they could place themselves under either their debtor as an indentured servant or another who could pay what they owed to their debtor. After they worked off the debt, their release would be granted.

In either case, this was a situation in which one person was under the full control of another and had to do what he was told. And at no time has this ever been a thing well received by our flesh. We naturally yearn to be free and not to be told what to do.

When you place all of that into the context of believers, things get even more complicated. Since many times believers would be indentured to other believers, while other times they would be indentured or even slaves to non-believers, how were they to react? In the first case, they would be indentured to other believers with whom they were absolutely equal in Christ. In the second case, they would be indentured or slaves to non-believers whose father was Satan while their own Father was God!

In either case, what were believing servants to do? Here is the command once again:

Colossians 3:22 *Servants, obey in all things your masters according to the flesh; not with eyeservice, as menpleasers; but in singleness of heart, fearing God:*

Once again, Acts 5:29 applies to this command, so yes, in rare and extreme cases, there would be limits as to how far this would go. No servant would be expected by God to slaughter the neighbors in their sleep just because their master said so.

But rare cases notwithstanding, servants were to obey their fleshly masters in all things. And while the Western world ended all forms of slavery and servitude long ago, the principles here apply very well to the employer/employee paradigm, at least while one is on the clock.

Servants were commanded to obey their masters *not with eyeservice, as menpleasers; but in singleness of heart, fearing God.* Not with eye service, as men-pleasers, meant not to simply do right while being watched, and not to do right just to try and be noticed. In our world, that is often exactly how employees operate, even believing employees. And for Christians, this was and is a horrible testimony. *In singleness of heart, fearing God,* means with sincerity and simplicity, having a reverence and respect for God who gave the command that they obey.

Colossians 3:23 *And whatsoever ye do, do it heartily, as to the Lord, and not unto men;* **24** *Knowing that of the Lord ye shall receive the reward of the inheritance: for ye serve the Lord Christ.*

Verse twenty-three is one of the most motivating verses in the Bible. But few likely realize that it was originally given not to free men, but to men in servitude. And if it was given to them in their often dire condition, how much more should we today be able and willing to obey it in our much more pleasant condition?

Whatever these servants did, they were to do it heartily, meaning from the depths of their souls. They were to do it as if it were God Himself who commanded it rather than a man. Can you imagine the testimony that Christians and churches would have if every believer worked like this?

But what could motivate a person under bonds to behave that well? Here again is the answer from Paul in verse twenty-four, *"Knowing that of the Lord ye shall receive the reward of the inheritance: for ye serve the Lord Christ."*

Would many believing servants in those days have to serve monster masters? Certainly. Do many believing Christians today have to work for boorish bosses? Absolutely. But in neither case will they be deprived of a full reward for their good work. God Himself, their real master, will fully reward them for every load carried, every meal cooked, every order taken, every package delivered, every toilet cleaned, every wire spliced, everything.

When you and I work with only our earthly bosses in view, we will probably work half-heartedly at best. But when we work with Christ our Lord in view, when we understand that we will answer to Him not just for our Sunday worship but for our Monday through Saturday work as well, and when we realize that He will reward soldering as well as soul winning and meal prep as well as missions, it will make us the best workers on earth.

Colossians 3:25 *But he that doeth wrong shall receive for the wrong which he hath done: and there is no respect of persons.*

It would be very easy to assume something absolutely backward about this verse, namely that this is a warning to the masters not to treat the servants wrongly. But masters are not being dealt with yet; that will begin in the next verse. This warning is to the servants, not to the masters. And the warning is that if a servant does wrong, God will punish him for it. God is not going to play favorites with him just because he is a believer.

You perhaps have an unbelieving and ill-behaving boss. You need to know that God is not going to give you a pass for bad behavior and shoddy work just because you are saved and they are not.

Do your job, and do it well.

Words for masters

Colossians 4:1 *Masters, give unto your servants that which is just and equal; knowing that ye also have a Master in heaven.*

This command has also been seen previously in Scripture:

Ephesians 6:9 *And, ye masters, do the same things unto them, forbearing threatening: knowing that your Master also is in heaven; neither is there respect of persons with him.*

Masters were/are commanded to give their servants that which is just and equal. Just is from the word *dikaion*, and it means righteous! Equal is from *isotayto,* and it means *fair and even.* So masters were to treat their servants, and employers are to treat their employees in a way that God Himself would be willing to put a "Righteous and Fair" label on.

And they are to do so *knowing that ye also have a Master in heaven.* In other words, you may be the boss, but you also have a boss. Others may answer to you, but you will have to answer to God.

I am all in favor of capitalism; it is the current economic system that most closely fulfills all the expectations of Scripture for a people. But when capitalism gets separated from righteousness, it makes people merely a means to an end, and that will *never* be approved of by the God who made man in His image and then died for all of us.

The bottom line is important, but it is not the only consideration. It is really not even the main consideration in God's sight. If any of us who employ others ignorantly imagine that God will, at the Judgment Seat of Christ, say, "Let me see your books so that I can pat you on the back if you squeezed every drop of profit out of people that you could without caring for them like I care for them," then we know nothing of Christ or Scripture. Yes, servants were to do their very best for their masters, but masters were to do their very best for their servants as well. Yes, Christian employees ought to be the best workers on earth, but Christian employers also ought to be the best bosses on earth.

People ought to be excited when they find out their boss is a Christian, not just because they know they will not be cursed or abused, but also because they know they will be paid righteously and fairly!

Paul has dealt with three sets of relationships: husband and wife, father and children, master and servants. But did you notice how all of those horizontal relationships with our fellow man tied in with our vertical relationship with God?

The Lord was mentioned five times. God was mentioned once. Christ was mentioned once. Master in Heaven was mentioned once. The way that we treat each other down here below impacts our fellowship with God above.

The outward affects the upward.

Chapter Eleven
Pray, Walk, and Talk

Colossians 4:2 *Continue in prayer, and watch in the same with thanksgiving;* **3** *Withal praying also for us, that God would open unto us a door of utterance, to speak the mystery of Christ, for which I am also in bonds:* **4** *That I may make it manifest, as I ought to speak.* **5** *Walk in wisdom toward them that are without, redeeming the time.* **6** *Let your speech be alway with grace, seasoned with salt, that ye may know how ye ought to answer every man.*

Having finished the outward and upward pairings of responsibility that he covered from Colossians 3:18-4:1, Paul will now use the remainder of the last chapter of the book to deal with many personal matters, as he is so prone to do. And these five verses will be marked by the simple words pray, walk, and talk.

A prayerful instruction

Colossians 4:2 *Continue in prayer, and watch in the same with thanksgiving;*

People who have been in church the bulk of their lives and read the Scripture for years often run the risk of skimming over things that the penman was really trying to emphasize. We see an instruction that we pray, and since there are so many instructions like that, we gloss over it.

Don't.

Paul's instruction that the Colossians and all believers continue in prayer was both important and emphatic. In fact, in the way Paul wrote it, the word order is flipped around to make prayer emphatic. It reads something like *the praying, continue in it.* And the word *continue* only adds to the emphasis. It is from the word *proskartereita*, and it means to be devoted to, to adhere to, to give unremitting attention to.

One thing that makes Paul's emphasis on prayer so interesting is that it is yet another instance in which we see that Paul and Jesus were constantly on the exact same page. We are often told that Paul contradicted Christ left and right, and nothing could be further from the truth. There was not so much as a millimeter of space between Christ and Paul on anything.

Here is how Jesus spoke about prayer:

Luke 18:1 *And he spake a parable unto them to this end, that men ought* ***always*** *to pray, and not to faint;*

Luke 21:36 *Watch ye therefore, and pray* ***always***...

Paul's imperative command that we continue in prayer is nothing more than a restatement of Christ's command that we always pray.

After commanding that believers continue in prayer, Paul added the additional instruction *and watch in the same.* Watch is from the word *graygoreuo,* and it means to give strict attention to, to be diligent, to be awake and paying attention. And once again, this is another instance of Paul and Jesus being on the exact same page on the subject. Here is how Jesus put it:

Matthew 26:41 *Watch and pray, that ye enter not into temptation: the spirit indeed is willing, but the flesh is weak.*

Watch is from the same root word in both texts. Both Christ our Lord and Paul the apostle, His servant, instructed us to be watchful and diligent in our praying. It is so incredibly easy to have our minds drift off to a thousand other things when we are trying to pray. It is even easy to find ourselves drifting into sleep as the apostles of Christ did in the garden of Gethsemane when He needed them to be praying the most!

Lazy praying will not likely bring life-changing results. Here is how James put it:

James 5:16b *...The effectual fervent prayer of a righteous man availeth much.*

So we are to continue in prayer, and we are to watch in prayer. But there was one additional word of instruction that Paul had for the Colossians on the subject:

Colossians 4:2 *Continue in prayer, and watch in the same <u>with thanksgiving</u>;*

Our diligent, watchful praying is to be praying with thanksgiving. Our prayers are never to devolve merely into a wish list as if God were some theological Santa Claus, nor are our prayers ever to be merely a complaint session as if the throne of heaven is some divine Yelp! review site for our disgruntled lives. Our prayers are to be saturated with thanksgiving because we always have so much for which to give thanks.

You would never want to see someone coming your way if all they ever did was complain or ask for things. Why should we expect God to enjoy such a thing, either?

In the very early days of our church, there were ten thousand pressures and just about as many heartaches. And there were also one or two people who absolutely, positively never had anything to say other than complaints, and I am not in the least exaggerating when I say that. If the phone rang and it was them, I knew beyond a doubt that I was about to get unloaded on.

And there were times when a day was already so incredibly stressful, and I heard the phone ring and saw their number pop up that I simply let it ring because I knew without question it was going to be the straw that broke the camel's back for the day.

But there were many other times when the day was already incredibly stressful, and I heard the phone ring and saw a different number or two pop up that I grabbed the phone like it was a lifeline thrown out to a drowning man because I knew the person on the other end was going to have something encouraging to say, usually something about how thankful they were for the Lord and the church.

There really is something to that.

Yes, present your needs and supplications to God. Yes, pour your heart out to God when you are hurting and broken. But do not forget to pray with thanksgiving because nothing is more appropriate based on how good God is to every one of us, and God loves to hear it.

But Paul is not quite done yet with the subject of prayer.

Colossians 4:3 *Withal praying also for us, that God would open unto us a door of utterance, to speak the mystery of Christ, for which I am also in bonds:* **4** *That I may make it manifest, as I ought to speak.*

Withal is one word, not two, and it is an old English word that has very much fallen out of use and thus bears some defining. It is from the word *hama,* and it simply means at the same time or along with that.

This, therefore, ties the instruction of verse three back to the instruction of verse two. So the thought runs something like this: continue in prayer, and watch in the same with thanksgiving, and at the same time, along with all that, be praying also for us.

And this was something that Paul never shied away from asking of others:

1 Thessalonians 5:25 *Brethren, pray for us.*

2 Thessalonians 3:1a *Finally, brethren, pray for us,*

Praying for others is supposed to be a substantial part of our prayer life. Both God and His choicest servants modeled that paradigm consistently:

Numbers 11:1 *And when the people complained, it displeased the LORD: and the LORD heard it; and his anger was kindled; and the fire of the LORD burnt among them, and consumed them that were in the uttermost parts of the camp.* **2** *And the people cried unto Moses; and when Moses prayed unto the LORD, the fire was quenched.*

1 Samuel 12:23 *Moreover as for me, God forbid that I should sin against the LORD in ceasing to pray for you: but I will teach you the good and the right way:*

Job 42:8 *Therefore take unto you now seven bullocks and seven rams, and go to my servant Job, and offer up for yourselves a burnt offering; and my servant Job shall pray for you: for him will I accept: lest I deal with you after your folly, in that ye have not spoken of me the thing which is right, like my servant Job.*

John 17:9 *I pray for them: I pray not for the world, but for them which thou hast given me; for they are thine.*

I could fill up an entire book with passages showing God and believers praying diligently for others. If our prayers are always and only for us, then we are not as much praying as we are politicking.

What is it, though, that Paul needed the Colossians to pray for on his behalf?

Here it is again:

Colossians 4:3 *Withal praying also for us, that God would open unto us a door of utterance, to speak the mystery of Christ, for which I am also in bonds:* **4** *That I may make it manifest, as I ought to speak.*

Paul specifically wanted the Colossians to pray that God would open a door of utterance for him and those with him to speak the mystery of Christ. A door of utterance is a euphemism that basically means an opportunity, an open door to speak.

Do remember that Paul was taking a very unpopular message to people who did not necessarily want to hear it and was being opposed the entire way by the Judaizers who did not want him to speak it. If he was going to have an opportunity to speak for Christ, it would have to be God opening the door for him to do so. And Paul was convinced that God would be more likely to open that door as a result of the prayers of His people.

This, by the way, should settle in your mind that Paul was not a Calvinist, and he did not believe that God foreordained everything. He very much believed that if people would pray, their prayers would actually make a difference. He believed that if enough people fervently prayed for a thing, God would be more likely to do that thing than if no one prayed or if a few people prayed lazily.

Your prayers do make a difference. Mind you, God did not have to do it that way. Had He so chosen, He absolutely could have foreordained everything and made our prayers pointless exercises in futility. But instead, since He so enjoys communication with His people, He allows His heart and His hand to be moved by our prayers to do things He otherwise would not.

As to what Paul intended to speak should that door be opened, verse three calls it *the mystery of Christ*. As in other references to the word mystery in the New Testament, this one means something that was hidden from view in times past but has now been made manifest. The mystery of Christ is simply the gospel, the fact that Jesus died on the cross for the sins of all mankind and that salvation is available to whoever will repent of sin and receive Christ as Lord and Savior.

This was the message that Paul wanted an open door to speak to everyone. And that is pretty fascinating since the very next phrase in verse three is *for which I am also in bonds*. Paul was right then in bondage for speaking that exact same message. And yet, rather than shutting up so he could be released, he was praying and asking others to pray that God would continue to open doors for him to speak the very words that had already gotten him into so much trouble.

Paul finished this section about prayer in verse four with the words, *That I may make it manifest, as I ought to speak*.

There is a unique and intentional pairing in verses three and four that we should take note of. Look at the two verses together once again:

Colossians 4:3 *Withal praying also for us, that God would open unto us a door of utterance, to speak the **mystery** of Christ, for which I am also in bonds:* **4** *That I may make it **manifest**, as I ought to speak.*

Mystery, manifest. Under the inspiration of the Holy Ghost, Paul chose his words beautifully here. Again, mystery meant something that had been hidden. Manifest means the exact opposite, something that is revealed and made visible. It was Paul's very correct understanding that the job of the New Testament Christian is to take the previously hidden truth about Christ and the gospel and make it visible for all the world to see and know. Paul said that this is how he *ought to speak*.

It is also how we ought to speak.

The gospel is not something that we are to be selective with, only sharing with a few; it is something that we are to proclaim to the entire world.

The gospel is not something that we are to be vague with, carefully couching our terms so as not to offend people; it is something we are to explain in perfect detail whether people get offended or not because it is the only way anyone can escape hell.

And all of this is something that Paul wanted believers to pray for diligently.

A purposeful walk

Colossians 4:5 *Walk in wisdom toward them that are without, redeeming the time.*

Paul's instruction to walk in wisdom is once more an imperative command, not a suggestion. And there is nothing mysterious or complicated in the wording; we are to behave ourselves wisely, we are to be prudent and discerning.

But the next phrase puts an important context to that imperative command. We are to walk in wisdom toward them that are without. Them that are without simply means the lost world around us, nonbelievers.

Why would Paul be so concerned that believers walk wisely in reference to their interactions with nonbelievers?

I think Albert Barnes gives the most accurate and practical list in reference to this. He said:

"One, men of the world judge of religion, not from the profession, but from the life of its friends.

Two, they judge of religion, not from preaching, or from books, or from the conduct of its Founder and his apostles, but from what they see in the daily walk and conversation of the members of the church.

Three, they understand the nature of religion so well as to know when its friends are or are not consistent with their profession.

Four, they set a much higher value on honesty and integrity than they do on the doctrines and duties of religion; and if the professed friends of religion are destitute of the principle of truth and honesty, they think they have nothing of any value. They may be very devout on the Sabbath; very regular at prayer-meetings; very strict, in the observance of rites and ceremonies--but all these are of little worth in the estimation of the world, unless attended with an upright life.

Five, no professing Christian can possibly do good to others who does not live an upright life. If you have cheated a man out of never so small a sum, it is vain that you talk to him about the salvation of his soul; if you have failed to pay him a debt when it was due, or to finish a piece of work when you promised it, or to tell him the exact truth in conversation, it is vain for you to endeavour to induce him to be a Christian. He will feel, if he does not say-- and he might very properly say--that he wants no religion which will not make a man honest.

Six, no man will attempt to do much good to others whose own life is not upright. He will be sensible of the inconsistency, and will feel that he cannot do it with any sense of propriety; and the honour of religion, therefore, and the salvation of our fellow-men, demand that, in all our intercourse with others, we should lead lives of the strictest integrity." (Barnes, 282)

All of that is excellent and accurate, and a perfect view, I think, of what Paul had in mind with his command that we walk wisely toward them there without, especially in light of the closing words of verse five, *redeeming the time.*

This word redeeming means to recover, to ransom, to make wise and sacred use of every opportunity to do good. In the context of what Paul is saying, our interactions with the world are to be so right and so godly that we do not waste time when we try to win them. If we are going to have to try to explain or excuse all of our bad behavior before we can get around to witnessing to someone, we are wasting time rather than redeeming it.

Our walk really does matter.

A powerful talk

Colossians 4:6 *Let your speech be alway with grace, seasoned with salt, that ye may know how ye ought to answer every man.*

Paul now brings us to an incredibly powerful and equally difficult verse. And do not let the word "let" at the beginning of the verse make you think that this is optional; this is another imperative command, not a suggestion.

We begin with the first phrase, *Let your speech be alway with grace*, or as we would put it in our modern vernacular, always with grace. It is from the word *pantoteh,* and it means at all times. Alway, always, at all times, let your speech be with grace. Grace, in this command, means kindness and goodwill.

Can you think of a more difficult command anywhere in Scripture? Because I personally cannot.

And yet, it is a command nonetheless.

Adam Clarke very much seems to have captured the spirit of what Paul had in mind in this command, saying, "A harsh method of proposing or defending the doctrines of Christianity only serves to repel men from those doctrines, and from the way of salvation." (Clarke, 532)

In other words, we are to tell the truth, but if we do so in a caustic and abrasive manner, we are going to push people away from that truth rather than draw them toward it. Remember, the previous verse opened the context of our dealing with the lost world. And that is still in mind here. Christians cannot afford to come across as hateful and insulting and belittling to those that they are supposedly trying to win.

Sadly, the most consistent violators of this command seem to be preachers rather than parishioners. There are things I have heard from the pulpits of camp meetings and jubilees and revivals that I cannot print in this book and would not speak to others. And while those hateful and off-color things whip up a frenzy and work up a crowd, they defy the command of this verse and push people away from Christ rather than draw them to Him.

Our speech is to be always with grace. William Burkitt observed, "The people wondered of old at the gracious words which came our of Christ's mouth; and we may justly wonder at the graceless words which come out of the mouths of many that are called Christians." (Linder)

Now, there is another side to that coin, and Paul quickly gives it:

Colossians 4:6 *Let your speech be alway with grace,* <u>*seasoned with salt*</u>*...*

Is our speech to always be with grace? Certainly. But does that mean it will always be *sweet*? Certainly not. Salt has a bite to it. Salt sometimes stings. Salt kills harmful things so that good things can be preserved. The fact that we are always to speak with grace does not mean that we are always required to say what people want to hear. And I am smiling as I write this, because I just got hung up on a few moments ago for saying what someone did not want to hear.

It was Saturday, May 4, 2024, at about 2 o'clock in the afternoon. I was in the church office working on this section of verses. The church phone rang, and Dana picked it up in her office. A moment later, she brought me the phone. And when she mouthed to me the name of the person the other end, I knew what was coming...

The "gentleman" on the other end has spent his entire life of three or four decades burning all of his bridges behind him and blaming everyone else in the world for his problems, especially his family. And now he has found himself (if he is telling the truth, which is always suspect) hundreds of miles from home and in need of money for a bus ticket.

He said, "My parents were really abusive, so I moved way up here to start a new life, and things didn't work out."

They never do for him. Anywhere. With anyone.

So now he is calling trying to get me to wire him money for a bus ticket back to North Carolina. Mind you, he has a father, a mother, a brother, a grandfather, a grandmother, and a bunch of cousins. And he has burned the bridges with every single one of them and blames it all on them. And at thirty-five-ish, he is whining about "abusive parents." A full-grown man!

My wife was listening to my end of the conversation as I talked with him. At my request, she always does when he calls so that I cannot easily be falsely accused as he has so falsely accused so many others. She does not mind, in fact, she finds it entertaining because she knows good and well I am going to get hung up on. He has very literally hung up on me more than any other human being on earth.

In a soothing voice and with utter kindness, with grace, as Paul commanded here, I said, "Bubba (not his real name), you really need to make things right with your parents; you have been estranged from them long enough, give them a call and be reconciled to them."

He hung up on me.

My speech was with grace – but it was also seasoned with salt. You are not required to tell people what they want to hear; you are merely required to tell them the truth with grace.

Paul ended verse six this way, *that ye may know how ye ought to answer every man.*

There is a right way to answer every statement and every question from every person. It may be different from person to person and circumstance to circumstance, but what will not be different is the guideline given that, on the one hand, our speech is to be marked with grace, and on the other hand, it is to be seasoned with salt.

Being saved will get us to heaven. But if we are going to make a difference on the way there, we need to pray right, walk right, and talk right!

Chapter Twelve
Name Dropping in the Best Way

Colossians 4:7 *All my state shall Tychicus declare unto you, who is a beloved brother, and a faithful minister and fellowservant in the Lord:* **8** *Whom I have sent unto you for the same purpose, that he might know your estate, and comfort your hearts;* **9** *With Onesimus, a faithful and beloved brother, who is one of you. They shall make known unto you all things which are done here.* **10** *Aristarchus my fellowprisoner saluteth you, and Marcus, sister's son to Barnabas, (touching whom ye received commandments: if he come unto you, receive him;)* **11** *And Jesus, which is called Justus, who are of the circumcision. These only are my fellowworkers unto the kingdom of God, which have been a comfort unto me.* **12** *Epaphras, who is one of you, a servant of Christ, saluteth you, always labouring fervently for you in prayers, that ye may stand perfect and complete in all the will of God.* **13** *For I bear him record, that he hath a great zeal for you, and them that are in Laodicea, and them in Hierapolis.* **14** *Luke, the beloved physician, and Demas, greet you.* **15** *Salute the brethren which are in Laodicea, and Nymphas, and the church which is in his house.* **16** *And when this epistle is read among you, cause that it be read also in the church of the Laodiceans; and that ye likewise read the epistle from Laodicea.* **17** *And say to Archippus, Take heed to the ministry which thou hast received in the Lord, that thou fulfil it.* **18** *The salutation by the hand of me Paul. Remember my bonds. Grace be with you. Amen. <Written from Rome to Colossians by Tychicus and Onesimus.>*

Paul was an academic—but Paul was not academic. And that is why his letters always seem to end on very personal notes.

Colossians will be no exception. And so, having written to people he had never met and yet deeply loved about important doctrinal issues, he devotes the last section of this epistle to some very encouraging name-dropping.

A treasury of names

Colossians 4:7 *All my state shall Tychicus declare unto you, who is a beloved brother, and a faithful minister and fellowservant in the Lord:* **8** *Whom I have sent unto you for the same purpose, that he might know your estate, and comfort your hearts;*

The words that Paul writes of Tychicus in verse seven are remarkably similar to the words he wrote of him in the Epistle to the Ephesians:

Ephesians 6:21 *But that ye also may know my affairs, and how I do, Tychicus, a beloved brother and faithful minister in the Lord, shall make known to you all things:*

Who was this Tychicus?

Here is what Scripture tells us.

Acts 20:4 *And there accompanied him into Asia Sopater of Berea; and of the Thessalonians, Aristarchus and Secundus; and Gaius of Derbe, and Timotheus; and of Asia, Tychicus and Trophimus.*

This is the first passage in Scripture in which we read of Tychicus. Paul has just come through a major uproar in Ephesus, he is now heading towards Macedonia, and the company going with him includes Tychicus of Asia, most likely from right there in Ephesus.

And then we read of him in Ephesians 6 as a trusted messenger from Paul back to the church at Ephesus:

Ephesians 6:21 *But that ye also may know my affairs, and how I do, Tychicus, a beloved brother and faithful minister in the Lord, shall make known to you all things:* **22** *Whom I have sent unto you for the same purpose, that ye might know our affairs, and that he might comfort your hearts.*

And then we read of him here in the epistle to the Colossians:

Colossians 4:7 *All my state shall Tychicus declare unto you, who is a beloved brother, and a faithful minister and fellowservant in the Lord:* **8** *Whom I have sent unto you for the same purpose, that he might know your estate, and comfort your hearts;*

Here, yet again, in our text we find Paul speaking of Tychicus in the most glowing of terms, calling him a beloved brother and a faithful minister and a fellow servant in the Lord, and entrusting him with a message to the church at Colosse.

Titus 3:12 *When I shall send Artemas unto thee, or Tychicus, be diligent to come unto me to Nicopolis: for I have determined there to winter.*

Here yet again we find Tychicus as a trusted messenger for Paul. Unlike so many in the life of Paul, nothing negative is ever said or inferred about Tychicus; each time we are introduced or reintroduced to him in Scripture, he is nothing but a blessing.

Every one of us should strive to be a Tychicus. It was Tychicus who would let the church at Colosse know everything that was going on with the apostle Paul and comfort their hearts. Paul knew that he could trust him to get the job done.

But Tychicus would not be alone in that task:

Colossians 4:9 *With Onesimus, a faithful and beloved brother, who is one of you. They shall make known unto you all things which are done here.*

Verse nine gives us a bit of "the rest of the story," as the late Paul Harvey would put it, of a different book of the Bible, the book of Philemon.

The book of Philemon was a personal letter written from Paul to Philemon, a friend, a man that he seems to have won to the Lord. Philemon had a slave who had run away and defrauded or outright stolen from him in the process. That slave's name was Onesimus – the very Onesimus that we are reading about here in Colossians.

When Onesimus ran away, he ran to the center of the world in that day, the enormous and populous city of Rome. It seems that he very much wanted to fade into the crowd so as to avoid detection. But he happened to run into a man named Paul – God is pretty good about things like that, and Onesimus got saved. Paul wrote the letter to Philemon to ask him to receive Onesimus back, not as a slave this time, but as a brother in the faith. He even agreed to pay Philemon whatever Onesimus owed him.

And he sent Onesimus back to Philemon carrying that letter.

But Onesimus also helped to bring the epistle to the Colossians as well at the exact same time. He and Tychicus together traveled with these precious documents in hand to deliver them.

In verse nine, Paul called Onesimus *a faithful and beloved brother, who is one of you*. So from the word brother, we learned that Onesimus was saved, and we also learn here that he was faithful and beloved, meaning that he could be counted on, and he had made himself dear to Paul and other believers. He was also "*one of you*," meaning that he was tied in with the people who made up the church of Colosse. He may have been actual family, or close friend, but they regarded him as one of them.

The end of verse nine lets us know that it would be Tychicus and Onesimus together that would bring the report on Paul to the church at Colosse.

Colossians 4:10a *Aristarchus my fellowprisoner saluteth you...*

I say so often that the big characters of Scripture get most of the preaching time and writing mentions, but the smaller characters of Scripture are often equally as interesting and instructive. And we meet another of those lesser-known characters here in verse ten, Aristarchus, whom Paul refers to as *my fellow prisoner*. Aristarchus was saluting, or as we would say, sending salutations to the church at Colosse along with Paul.

So, who was this Aristarchus?

We first read of him in Acts 19:

Acts 19:23 *And the same time there arose no small stir about that way.* **24** *For a certain man named Demetrius, a silversmith, which made silver shrines for Diana, brought no small gain unto the craftsmen;* **25** *Whom he called together with*

134

the workmen of like occupation, and said, Sirs, ye know that by this craft we have our wealth. **26** *Moreover ye see and hear, that not alone at Ephesus, but almost throughout all Asia, this Paul hath persuaded and turned away much people, saying that they be no gods, which are made with hands:* **27** *So that not only this our craft is in danger to be set at nought; but also that the temple of the great goddess Diana should be despised, and her magnificence should be destroyed, whom all Asia and the world worshippeth.* **28** *And when they heard these sayings, they were full of wrath, and cried out, saying, Great is Diana of the Ephesians.* **29** *And the whole city was filled with confusion: and having caught Gaius and* **Aristarchus**, *men of Macedonia, Paul's companions in travel, they rushed with one accord into the theatre.*

While in Macedonia, some men had apparently believed on Christ and joined the apostle Paul's mission work. Aristarchus was one of those men. And when they got to Ephesus, so many people were won to the Lord and forsaking the worship of Diana that the local craftsmen, who made a nice profit building small shrines to Diana, stirred up a mob against them.

Paul did not get caught up in this mob, but Gaius and Aristarchus did. They got forced into the arena and were legitimately at risk of losing their lives. For most people, that kind of thing would be enough to induce an immediate "career change." But Aristarchus was not most people. Let's check in on Paul and company again more than three months after the uproar in Ephesus:

Acts 20:4 *And there accompanied him into Asia Sopater of Berea; and of the Thessalonians, Aristarchus and Secundus; and Gaius of Derbe, and Timotheus; and of Asia, Tychicus and Trophimus.*

There Aristarchus is again, still traveling and serving with Paul in spite of nearly losing his life in Ephesus! And he just kept on doing that:

Acts 27:1 *And when it was determined that we should sail into Italy, they delivered Paul and certain other prisoners unto one named Julius, a centurion of Augustus' band.* **2** *And entering into a ship of Adramyttium, we launched, meaning to* *sail by the coasts of Asia; one Aristarchus, a Macedonian of Thessalonica, being with us.*

Roughly three or four years pass between Acts 20 and Acts 27, and Aristarchus is still with Paul, this time sailing for Rome with him. By the way, he does not realize it, but he is about to go through an epic storm, Euroclydon, a shipwreck, and nearly be drowned with Paul on this trip. And yet, the next thing we read, he is in Rome with Paul and is actually, at least for a time, a fellow prisoner alongside Paul.

Paul did not mind name-dropping Aristarchus; the man was loyal and beloved and for very good reason.

Colossians 4:10b... *and Marcus, sister's son to Barnabas, (touching whom ye received commandments: if he come unto you, receive him;)*

Not only did Aristarchus want to salute the believers at Colosse, Marcus, or as we usually refer to him, Mark, John Mark, did as well. This is the same relative of Barnabas that Paul and Barnabas broke fellowship over in Acts 15. He had been with Paul and Barnabas on a previous missionary journey and bailed out along the way. So when it came time for a different missionary journey, Barnabas, the relative, wanted to give him another chance, and Paul did not.

And this was not some "kindly agree to disagree" situation:

Acts 15:39 *And the contention was so sharp between them, that they departed asunder one from the other: and so Barnabas took Mark, and sailed unto Cyprus;*

To be blunt, everyone here blew it, everyone was in the wrong, and this was simply an ugly disaster. And yet, years later, people have cooled down and rethought things, Mark has obviously matured a great deal, and he is now with Paul again in the service. And it is very likely that well-publicized past that led to Paul writing the words at the end of verse ten, *(touching whom ye received commandments: if he come unto you, receive him;)*.

This seems very much to have been Paul saying something akin to, "Yes, everything you heard about Mark bailing out on us was true; but that was a long time ago. All is forgiven, he is different, he is helpful to me in the ministry, so do as you have been commanded and receive him if he comes."

Colossians 4:11 *And Jesus, which is called Justus, who are of the circumcision. These only are my fellowworkers unto the kingdom of God, which have been a comfort unto me.*

It almost seems somehow wrong to us to see the name Jesus in Scripture and realize that it does not apply to THE Jesus. But one of the very wonders of Jesus becoming the name above all names is that it was actually a somewhat common name in Bible days. In fact, there is another instance in Scripture in which someone else also carried the name Jesus:

Hebrews 4:8 *For if Jesus had given them rest, then would he not afterward have spoken of another day.*

This Jesus was the Joshua of the Old Testament.

The Jesus of Colossians 4:11 also bore the surname Justus. There are two other mentions of a Justus in the New Testament, but neither of them seems to be the same as this Jesus Justus.

Of this man we are simply told in verse eleven that he, along with Mark and Aristarchus were *of the circumcision,* meaning that they were Jewish believers, and that these three *only are my fellowworkers unto the kingdom of God, which have been a comfort unto me.*

When he singles them out as being the only ones who were his fellow workers and which had been a comfort to him, take that in the context of what he just said about them being of the circumcision. Of the Jews, they were the only three in Rome that were on this list. Other Gentiles have already been mentioned and will continue to be mentioned as being with him as fellow workers and comforters. But of the Jews, it was just these three.

Colossians 4:12 *Epaphras, who is one of you, a servant of Christ, saluteth you, always labouring fervently for you in prayers, that ye may stand perfect and complete in all the will of God.* **13** *For I bear him record, that he hath a great zeal for you, and them that are in Laodicea, and them in Hierapolis.*

Back in chapter one of Colossians, we were introduced to Epaphras. We learned Epaphras was likely the one who first preached the gospel to the Colossians and saw many of them saved and a church started. We observed that Epaphras later became the tie-in between Paul and the Colossians and a fellow servant with Paul in the ministry. For the Colossians, he was a *faithful minister of Christ*. And the word used here for minister is from the same word that we get the word deacon from, and indicates one who is a servant.

So Epaphras did not just preach the gospel to them, he ministered to them, and he built a deep rapport with them through that. We also learned in Colossians 1:8 that it was Epaphras who *"declared unto us* [Paul and those who were with him in Rome] *your love in the Spirit."*

And now as he begins to bring the epistle to a close, Paul references Epaphras once again, saying that he is both *one of you,* meaning of Colosse, and *a servant of Christ.* Like those mentioned before him, Epaphras wanted to salute the church at Colosse, and additionally, Paul said that he, Epaphras, was *always labouring fervently for you in prayers, that ye may stand perfect and complete in all the will of God.*

Paul knew Epaphras to be a praying man, and to be one who especially labored over the Colossians in prayer, touching heaven constantly and asking God to help them, the Colossians, stand perfect and complete in all the will of God.

That is an interesting and instructive prayer. He was not praying that they would stand perfect and complete in their position before God; that was fully settled when they got saved and God imputed His righteousness to their account. What was not settled at salvation, what is never settled at salvation, is whether or not a person or church full of people will stand perfect and complete in all the will of God.

This prayer was not about whether they were going to heaven; it was about whether they were doing the will of God on the way there.

And Epaphras was praying for them to be absolutely perfect and complete and that.

We should be laboring fervently in prayer over the same thing for ourselves and for others.

Paul is not yet quite done writing about Epaphras. Look at verse thirteen once more:

Colossians 4:13 *For I bear him record, that he hath a great zeal for you, and them that are in Laodicea, and them in Hierapolis.*

Epaphras was not halfhearted and lukewarm about other believers. Paul worded this in such a way as if to indicate he would be willing to stand as a legal witness to the great zeal that Epaphras had for the believers there in Colosse but also for the believers in Laodicea and Heirapolis, two other towns in the same region. So not only was Epaphras not halfhearted and lukewarm about other believers, he was also not concerned merely with those in his own hometown; his zeal extended to other towns, and he traveled far afield with Paul as they together tried to win the world.

Colossians 4:14 *Luke, the beloved physician, and Demas, greet you.*

Luke was a long-term traveling companion of Paul, the author of the Gospel of Luke and the book of Acts, a Gentile by birth though likely a proselyte to Judaism before getting saved, and, as described here, *the beloved physician.*

Demas is mentioned here as well as sending greetings to the church in Colosse along with Luke. He will later rather famously forsake the Apostle Paul because he loved the world more than he loved the Lord.

As for this mention of Luke, though, it is fascinating to consider Paul calling him the beloved physician. Do remember that Paul miraculously healed numbers of people, especially in the early days of his ministry, and even brought Eutychus back from the dead. Later, though, Paul, who is described as having a thorn in the flesh, seemingly is described as being nearly blind, had his body mangled when a mob stoned him, and was beaten with rods, refers to Luke as the beloved physician. It seems as if in the years when the sign gifts were beginning to cease, Luke stepped in to do what he could medically do to alleviate Paul's pain and keep him functioning.

One thing is very clear from this: solid faith and good medicine are allies, not adversaries.

A trading of letters

Colossians 4:15 *Salute the brethren which are in Laodicea, and Nymphas, and the church which is in his house.*

There was a church in Colosse, and there was a church down the road in Laodicea. Paul wanted those churches to salute each other; he wanted them to be on good terms. And this is a good reminder for today; Bible believing churches are allies, not adversaries.

Paul also wanted the Colossians to salute a man named Nymphas, and the church which was in his house. This is the only place in Scripture that we read of him, and the only thing we know about this man who was clearly a believer is that he had opened his home to serve as a place for the church to meet together. The temple was no longer an option, the synagogues were no longer an option, and it would be a while in many locations before churches were able to have their own dedicated properties and buildings in which to meet. People like Nymphas bridged the gap by opening their homes to meet the current need.

Colossians 4:16 *And when this epistle is read among you, cause that it be read also in the church of the Laodiceans; and that ye likewise read the epistle from Laodicea.*

Being in reasonably close proximity, Paul instructed that the Colossians read their own epistle and then send it to the Laodiceans so they could read it as well, and that the Laodiceans read their epistle and send it to the Colossians so that they could read it.

Obviously, only one of those two epistles was chosen by God to be part of the inspired Scripture. But it is still interesting to consider that Paul and the early church wanted Scripture circulated and read by everyone. They very early on understood the importance of the written Word of God.

It is also interesting to consider, though, that though we do not have access to the epistle to the Laodiceans, we know that they read the Epistle to the Colossians. And we also know that they did not take very good heed to it. And the reason we know that is because of another letter that was written to them maybe thirty-five years later:

Revelation 3:14 *And unto the angel of the church of the Laodiceans write; These things saith the Amen, the faithful and true witness, the beginning of the creation of God;* **15** *I know thy works, that thou art neither cold nor hot: I would thou wert cold or hot.* **16** *So then because thou art lukewarm, and neither cold nor hot, I will spue thee out of my mouth.* **17** *Because thou sayest, I am rich, and increased with goods, and have need of nothing; and knowest not that thou art wretched, and miserable, and poor, and blind, and naked:* **18** *I counsel thee to buy of me gold tried in the fire, that thou mayest be rich; and white raiment, that thou mayest be clothed, and that the shame of thy nakedness do not appear; and anoint thine eyes with eyesalve, that thou mayest see.* **19** *As many as I love, I rebuke and chasten: be zealous therefore, and repent.* **20** *Behold, I stand at the door, and knock: if any man hear my voice, and open the door, I will come in to him, and will sup with him, and he with me.* **21** *To him that overcometh will I grant to sit with me in my throne, even as I also overcame, and am set down with my Father in his throne.* **22** *He that hath an ear, let him hear what the Spirit saith unto the churches.*

The Laodiceans were able to read the Epistle to the Colossians, which told them in verse eighteen of chapter one that in all things He, Christ, was to have the preeminence. And yet by the time John the Apostle wrote to them not many years later, Christ is picturing Himself as standing outside the door of that church and knocking and asking to be allowed to come in.

The entire book of Colossians that the Laodiceans read was about the deity of Christ and our duty to put Him first in all things. And yet, so very few years later, Christ is so sick of them that He intends to spew them out of His mouth.

Clearly, merely having access to the Scripture does not mean we have actually absorbed or applied Scripture.

A trust for Archippus

Colossians 4:17 *And say to Archippus, Take heed to the ministry which thou hast received in the Lord, that thou fulfil it.*

Archippus is mentioned twice in Scripture, here and in Philemon 1:2 where Paul calls him "our fellow soldier." From what Paul says of him here in Colossians, it is clear that he had been called to the ministry in some capacity. And Paul was reminding him to take heed to it and to fulfill it.

We do not know what or where that ministry was; we do know that Paul wanted him to regard it as a sacred trust and truly give himself to it.

A tender conclusion

Colossians 4:18 *The salutation by the hand of me Paul. Remember my bonds. Grace be with you. Amen. <Written from Rome to Colossians by Tychicus and Onesimus.>*

This closing verse of the Epistle opens a window to us and allows us to see some tender and precious things. First of all, we find that verse eighteen is the only one that Paul wrote with his own hand. And this is not the only time we find something like this:

1 Corinthians 16:21 *The salutation of me Paul with mine own hand.*

2 Thessalonians 3:17 *The salutation of Paul with mine own hand, which is the token in every epistle: so I write.*

Paul signed his own name in every single epistle he wrote. And his handwriting was evidently very recognizable.

But why would it be like this? The most logical supposition is because Paul was nearly blind by this point, as Galatians 4:15 seems to hint. So he used penmen to write the epistles as he dictated them. And in this case, he used the same two men who would be carrying that epistle to the Colossians, Tychicus and Onesimus.

But look now at his final words before he mentioned his penmen:

Remember my bonds. Grace be with you. Amen.

Grace be with you was very common in Paul's writings and in Paul's closings, as was the word amen. But this is the one and only time he ever wrote the words *Remember my bonds*.

To the church full of people that He had never seen face-to-face and who had never seen him face-to-face, he said, *Remember my bonds*. He writes this entire epistle, this doctrinal treatise on the deity of Christ to combat the heresy of the Gnostics, and he ends it by saying, "Remember my bonds."

The Gnostics had some very polished philosophy. The Gnostics were very popular. The Gnostics were very academic.

But the Gnostics were paying no price whatsoever for what they were trying to teach the Colossians.

Paul so very much believed in the deity of Christ that he was that very moment in bonds for it.

No wonder God has preserved the Epistle to the Colossians for 2,000 years now, has had it translated into hundreds of world languages, and has had it read by billions and billions of people the world over, while the writings of the Gnostics are somewhere near the bottom of the dustbin of literary history.

Works Cited

Barnes, A. (1996). *Barnes' notes* (Vol. 12). Baker.

Clarke, A. (1977). *The Holy Bible, containing the Old and New Testaments, the text carefully printed from the most correct copies of the present authorized translation, including the marginal readings and parallel texts: With a commentary and critical notes designed as a help to a better understanding of the sacred writings* (Vol. 6). Abingdon Press.

Lindner, P. (2003). Power Bible CD Version (5.9). *Power Bible.*, https://powerbible.com/. 2010/09/14.

Parker, C., & Westfall, S. (2021, August 3). For some athletes, the olympics aren't just a chance to compete — they're an opportunity to defect claire parker and sammy westfall. *Washington Post*. Retrieved September 20, 2024, from https://www.washingtonpost.com/world/2021/08/02/olympic-defectors-history/.

Qurollo, J. A. (2008). *Notes on Colossians and Philemon.* Qurollo Publishing.

Henry, M. (n.d.). *Matthew Henry's commentary on the whole Bible* (Vol. 6). Fleming H. Revell Co.

Other Books by Dr. Wagner

Daniel: Breathtaking
Ephesians: The Treasures of Family
Esther: Five Feasts and the Fingerprints of God
Galatians: The Treasures of Liberty
James: The Pen and the Plumb Line
Jonah: A Story of Greatness
Nehemiah: A Labor of Love
Philippians: The Treasures of Joy
Proverbs Vol 1: Bright Light from Dark Sayings
Proverbs Vol 2: Bright Light from Dark Sayings
The Revelation: Ready or Not
Romans: Salvation from A-Z
Ruth: Diamonds in the Darkness
Beyond the Colored Coat
From Footers to Finish Nails
Learning Not to Fear the Old Testament
Marriage Makers/Marriage Breakers
I'm Saved! Now What???
Don't Muzzle the Ox

Books in the Night Heroes Series
Cry from the Coal Mine (Vol 1)
Free Fall (Vol 2)
Broken Brotherhood (Vol 3)
The Blade of Black Crow (Vol 4)
Ghost Ship (Vol 5)
When Serpents Rise (Vol 6)
Moth Man (Vol 7)
Runaway (Vol 8)
Terror by Day (Vol 9)
Winter Wolf (Vol 10)

Desert Heat (Vol 11)
Deadline (Vol 12)

Other Fiction

Zak Blue: Falcon Wing
Zak Blue: Enter the Maelstrom

Devotionals

DO Drops Vol. 1
DO Drops Vol. 2
DO Drops Vol. 3
DO Drops Vol. 4
DO Drops Vol. 5
DO Drops Vol. 6
DO Drops Vol. 7
DO Drops Vol. 8
DO Drops Vol. 9
DO Drops Vol 10
DO Drops Vol 11
DO Drops Vol. 12

www.ingramcontent.com/pod-product-compliance
Lightning Source LLC
Chambersburg PA
CBHW060156070426
42447CB00033B/1667